Encyclopedia of
Wood Joints

Encyclopedia of
Wood Joints

The Taunton Press

**Wolfram
Graubner**

Cover photo: Susan Kahn

Photos on pp. 34, 41 (middle), 45 (top), 51 (top and bottom) and 107 courtesy of John Weatherhill, Inc., New York and Tokyo.

Joint construction by master carpenter Fumio Tanaka, Tokyo; Firma Hotzenholz, Herrischried; the students of the Vocational Training School, Munich; and staff at The Taunton Press.

TAUNTON
BOOKS & VIDEOS

...by fellow enthusiasts

© 1992 by The Taunton Press, Inc.
All rights reserved.

First published in Germany as
*Holzverbindungen:
Gegenüberstellungen japanischer und
europäischer Lösungen*
(© 1986 Deutsche Verlags-Anstalt GmbH, Stuttgart)

A FINE WOODWORKING Book

FINE WOODWORKING® is a trademark of The Taunton Press, Inc.,
registered in the U.S. Patent and Trademark Office.

The Taunton Press, 63 South Main Street, Box 5506,
Newtown, CT 06470-5506

Library of Congress Cataloging-in-Publication Data

Graubner, Wolfram.
     [Holzverbindungen. English]
     Encyclopedia of Wood Joints / Wolfram Graubner
          p.   cm.
     "A Fine Woodworking book"—T.p. verso.
     ISBN 1-56158-004-X
     1. Woodwork.   2. Timber joints.   3. Joinery I. Title.
TT185.G76613   1992   91-38456
684'.08—dc20   CIP

My thanks for their cooperation to Naomi Okawa (Tokyo),
Kiyoshi Seike (Tokyo), Kiyoshi Miyazaki (Chiba)
and Manfred Speidel (Aachen).

For their encouragement while working on this book,
I thank Hugo Kükelhaus (Soest) and Fritz Gotthelf (Munich),
both of whom died in 1984.

—*Wolfram Graubner*

Contents

Introduction

To understand the 600 or so wood joints known to us today, it is important to grasp a few basic principles. Different joint forms were not developed exclusively for a particular function, and it is not self-evident which joint should be used in which part of a construction. The great majority of wood joints came into existence as generations of craftsmen developed and adapted existing joints in response to changing conditions and demands. In this way, simple lap joints and mortise-and-tenon joints have evolved into complex joint forms that can withstand stresses from all sides.

Joints are made where supporting and supported elements meet, where timbers must be spliced together, supported or braced and where boards have to be joined together, secured to prevent warp or assembled to make a carcase. Every cultural region has developed its own particular joinery in response to the conditions and requirements of the time. Thus, in Japan we find sophisticated joints for splicing wood along its length, but only a few oblique joints. The Japanese try to avoid diagonal bracing in wooden buildings, because it doesn't provide sufficient elasticity to withstand earthquakes. To give buildings their necessary rigidity, long construction timbers must be used, and posts and beams must be fastened in such a way that they resist tension and compression. These methods of construction led to the overexploitation of tall trees as early as the 11th and 12th centuries in Japan, which meant that it became necessary to use short and crooked trees for construction timbers instead. Splicing joints had to be used to get the lengths necessary for beams. Southern European wood construction in the Roman tradition developed in a different direction. Extensive cross-bracing necessitated the use of many angled joints, whereas splicing joints were seldom used in European timber-frame structures.

The branching forms of trees served as the earliest models for wood joints, but it was the human hand that made it possible to test various clasping, grasping and interlocking movements. We can follow the evolution of wood joints through the history of tools. Splitting tools, such as the ax, the wedge, the drawknife and the adz, appeared in the distant past. Tongue-and-groove joinery, which is used widely in the wood industry today, is one of the oldest methods for joining stock edge to edge. By splitting round stock it was possible to make triangular openings, on the broad side of which a drawknife was used to make the groove. The acute-angled side was then inserted in the groove.

Improvements in tools made possible a number of decorative variations on basic wood joints. At the same time, there was a constant effort to find ways to make joints tighter fitting, stronger and less visible. The result was sophisticated joinery, visible from the outside only through oblique mitered cuts, which, in the best cases, were hidden by the wood's figure.

With the development of steel, concrete and other uniform construction materials and the widespread use of metal fasteners, traditional methods of wood joinery have, to a certain extent, fallen into obscurity. Similarly, much of the expression in design by cabinetmakers has been lost because furniture is now constructed mainly with manufactured sheet materials and glue joints.

In spite of these developments, the stability of traditional wood joints has not been surpassed and wood joints remain the mark of quality construction and cabinetmaking. The specific characteristics of wood—a material that reacts differently along its length than across its width or thickness—are clearly different from more uniform materials. It is therefore essential to take into consideration wood's varying strength and its reaction to forces from different directions when choosing joints. The different rates of shrinkage along the length and width of a board makes it particularly important to take precautions when joining end grain to edge grain. End grain, which is especially susceptible to decay, demands measures of protection when it is exposed.

The joints that are presented in this book are the result of practical experience in carpentry and cabinetmaking. I hope that the joints will give you a greater appreciation for the beauty and function of traditional wood joinery and also encourage you to reproduce the joints in your own workshop. And, in the best traditions of wood joinery, perhaps you will be encouraged to refine some of them to suit your own particular needs.

Wood Joints vs. Metal Fasteners

The metalworking industry developed bar-like metal fasteners for wood construction at the beginning of the 20th century. In the 1950s, at which time there was a great demand for houses and apartments, various types of steel plates for joining beams came onto the market. Since that time, metal fasteners have increasingly taken the place of traditional methods of wood joinery. After several decades of experience with metal fasteners, it is possible to assess the effectiveness of metal-to-wood joinery versus wood-to-wood joinery.

The extensive analyses and comprehensive tables of load-bearing capacity compiled by the manufacturers of metal fasteners are invaluable for planners and architects. Comparable load tables are not available to the same extent for wood joinery. The research necessary to produce such tables would be prohibitively expensive for individual carpentry firms to finance, and, to date, public institutions have provided little financial support.

Further advantages of metal fasteners lie in their easy assembly and manageable calculation. Master carpenters no longer have to rely on skilled workers for the assembly of metal fasteners.

On the other hand, the production of metal fasteners is not necessarily less expensive than the production of wood-to-wood joints. Moreover, the metalworking industry, which is one of the heaviest consumers of energy, puts great strains on the environment.

Traditional wood joinery has evolved through hundreds of years of experience, constantly improving and encompassing the best ways to use the unique qualities of wood. The disadvantages of wood lie, in part, in its weakness in cross section, a fault that can be compensated by appropriate methods corresponding to the special features of the material. With the advent of steel construction and codes of structural safety during the middle of the 19th century, several excellent methods of wood construction, such as arched beams, disappeared, because they could not be calculated exactly. In Switzerland there are wooden bridges constructed during the 18th century according to this technique that still withstand the strain of today's heavy traffic.

The stability of wooden joinery is more easily verified through experimentation than through calculation. Something made from wood must be considered in its entirety, because wood reacts in an elastic way and loads are distributed at individual points.

Fire and Wooden Joinery

Effective fire protection involves both measures taken to prevent outbreaks of fire and measures to avert the dangers that threaten after a fire has begun. In recent years, the emphasis has been on finding building methods that can increase the amount of time a building can remain standing during a fire. Building codes require that the superstructure of buildings be designed to resist fire long enough to give ample time to evacuate people, without endangering the lives of firefighters and rescue personnel. Fires often have catastrophic consequences because a building collapses during the early stages of a fire.

All building materials, whether they are combustible or noncombustible, are damaged by fire. Wood structures can have a prolonged resistance to fire only if all their structural parts, even the weakest, conform to the required standards. Metal fasteners between the beams in wood structures have proven to be the weak spots.

Recent studies in the wake of catastrophic fires have clearly demonstrated that metal fasteners do not offer sufficient security, even at the lowest level of fire-resistance standards. During a fire, exposed metal fasteners become red hot after only 15 to 25 minutes, causing structural failure at the joints and subsequent collapse of the building.

Even if metal fasteners are mounted in holes in the wood and are therefore not directly exposed to the flames, they still become red hot and burn the wood around them, because they are good conductors of heat. Their ability to keep members clamped together is quickly lost. Studies stress that metal fasteners should be used only when they are covered with wood or protected by fire shields. We can conclude that wood-to-wood joints guarantee burning buildings a longer resistance to collapse than do metal-to-wood joints. Only the latest fire-safety codes take into account the advantages of joints made solely of wood.

Wood normally ignites at temperatures between 300°C and 500°C (550°F to 900°F). The temperature on the burning wood's surface reaches 1,100°C (2,000°F). However, the subsequent charring of the wood's surface has an insulating effect, which lowers the temperature and retards further combustion, sometimes even preventing it. In addition, wood's poor thermal conductivity prevents the transfer of heat from a timber's surface to its core.

The buildup of heat forces the water out of the wood, which increases its strength. Thus, the damage to the outer part of the wood is compensated for by the increased load-bearing capacity of the wood's interior.

Steel girders, deformed by intense heat and wrenched from their substructure as a result of thermal expansion

All building materials are deformed when subjected to temperature changes. For example, steel beams can become so distorted that they break away from the supporting substructure. By contrast, the distortion of wood when subjected to heat is minimal, not least because the release of moisture causes the wood to shrink. For this reason, even at high temperatures wood construction members exert little tension at points of attachment.

Unlike structures made of heat-conducting materials, wood structures develop a protective shell during combustion. Wood near the source of the fire provides a shield that delays ignition of structural members beyond it. By contrast, metal structural members disperse heat quickly, which leads to the rapid spread of the fire or deformation of other parts of the structure.

Timbers can withstand fire for one and a half hours or more. The period of resistance can be increased by using hardwood. A few timbers with large cross-sectional dimensions are better than many timbers with small dimensions.

Timbers selected for construction should be planed and chamfered and have as few cracks and splits as possible. The latter can be avoided by using winter-cut timber that has no heartwood. The appropriate methods of cutting are discussed further on p. 8.

Methods of construction that allow at least 3 m (10 ft.) between wood supporting walls and no more than 3 m (10 ft.) between stories further contribute to protection against fires.

The risk of fire spreading rapidly is greatest in small rooms with high ceilings. This is because the closer the walls are to each other, the greater the risk that radiant heat from the center of the fire will cause the walls to catch fire spontaneously. Wood does not usually ignite from mere contact with fire but from a buildup of heat. When on fire, rooms with high ceilings act as chimneys. Hot air rises fast and creates a draft that feeds the fire with oxygen.

Wood Protection

Wood is subject to a natural cycle of growth and decay, unless special measures are taken to interrupt the cycle. Nature provides the fungi, insects and bacteria that destroy wood. However, certain conditions must exist for these enemies of wood to begin their destructive work. High humidity and warm temperatures are necessary for the development of fungi. Insects and their larvae feed on the starch contained in wood, and they lay their eggs in cracks in the wood. Effective wood protection must prevent the conditions that favor attacks by fungi and insects. Certain species of wood contain natural poisons in their heartwood, such as thujaplicin, that repel insects and larvae. Conifers, oak, sandalwood, camphor trees and ebony are some of the trees with this natural protection. Chestnut, larch, oak, pine and cherry contain substances in their heartwood that inhibit the development of fungi.

Metal fasteners and condensation

Wood is an above-average insulator compared to many inorganic building materials. Wood's insulating effect is greater across the grain than with the grain and is more pronounced in light, dry wood than in dense wood.

Problems arise when metal fasteners penetrate wooden beams in unheated rooms. Because metal is a good conductor of heat, metal fasteners cool much faster than the surrounding wood when there is a change of temperature. According to the laws of physics, water vapor always moves from a warm surface to a cold surface, which is why condensation often forms on cold metal fasteners. As a result, metal fasteners rust where their galvanized coating has been damaged by abrasion upon entering the wood. In addition, the wood surrounding the fasteners rots because it is continually damp. When this happens, bolts no longer hold firmly and they lose their load-bearing function.

To delay the process of decay, large quantities of chemical wood preservatives are often used, which would be unnecessary in a building made entirely with wood-to-wood joints. Unfortunately, the beams are invariably treated along their entire length instead of just at those points where it is really necessary, that is, in the holes drilled for the fasteners.

Joints secured with bolts that have a certain amount of play rapidly loose their seat as the process of decay begins. By contrast, nails actually seat better in the wood, at least for a while, because their friction fit is improved by the buildup of rust and shrinkage of the wood.

Sugi *wood (cedar)*

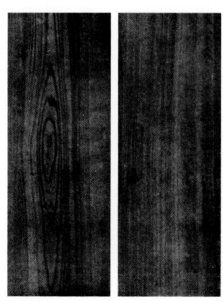

Hiuki *wood (cypress)*

Species of wood used in construction

Effective wood protection depends on the choice of species best suited to meet the demands of a particular part of a building or piece of furniture.

By tradition, Japanese carpenters use several different species of wood in a single building.

Cypress *(Chamae cyparis)* is extremely resistant to all kinds of parasites, and Japanese building codes currently in force do not require that it be treated. Because cypress is expensive, it is used only where timbers are under great stress.

Japanese **hiba** wood *(Thujopsis dellabrata)* is similar to cypress and has regular growth with few knots.

Although it is not as decay resistant or as strong as cypress, **hemlock** is the wood most commonly used in construction.

Trunks of **red pine,** which are often crooked, are still used today in their natural state for roof trusses.

Oak and **maple** are used to make loose tenons and splines and the many different kinds of wedges and treenails used in joinery.

If many joints must be worked on the same member, hardwood is favored because its close-grained structure facilitates precise work. Preferred species are **mulberry** and **paulownia.**

Imported woods such as **sandalwood, ebony** and **ironwood** are highly prized for wall shelving and alcoves.

Bamboo is the choice for rafters, lath, latticework and fences.

The range of wood used in European construction is much more modest.

Spruce has many uses, and although it is not particularly decay resistant it is stable. For this reason, it is now used instead of pine for window frames. **Pine** is more resistant to decay, but it tends to warp in the sun.

Larch is particularly resistant to decay and has good elasticity. However, there is very little larch left in Europe, and what is available often contains reaction wood.

Fir is often very wet, has wide growth rings and brown coloration, and because it often contains reaction wood, is difficult to plane. Even though fir is available in large diameters and contains little resin, furniture makers and carpenters alike usually avoid using it. Nevertheless, foresters continue to plant fir trees because they grow quickly, have solid footing in unfavorable conditions (in wet soils and exposed to the wind) and can flourish in the shade of larger trees.

Douglas-fir also has its disadvantages: The wood is heavy and has many large, hard knots that chip when planed.

Oak is the only wood that has a wide range of applications in European construction, notably for structural members under stress and substructure. Cabinetmakers also like to use hardwood, especially fruit woods.

Unlike their Japanese counterparts, Western craftsmen typically use only one or two different species of wood in a building or a piece of furniture. Consequently, tensions within the structure caused by the different rates of shrinkage of different species of wood are of much less significance than in Japanese wood construction.

Tree selection and harvesting

When selecting wood for a particular purpose, it is important to take into account the site where trees are grown. In the West, as in Japan, trees that grow on southeast-facing slopes are preferred for coniferous wood. Conifers that do not grow straight or are exposed to wind from one direction develop compression, or reaction, wood toward the underside of the leaning stem. Hardwoods, by contrast, develop tension wood on the upper, protected side of the trunk. These zones of tension and compression make the wood abnormally hard and, consequently, difficult to work. Reaction wood is also prone to checking and splitting. Trees that grow on gentle slopes facing southeast in closed-in wooded areas seem to be the best protected, and produce wood with even and gentle growth.

So called dry stands—standing, dead trees—yield wood that is greatly prized by cabinetmakers (if wood-boring beetles don't get there first). Special techniques have been devised in both the East and the West to produce this type of wood artificially. It used to be the custom in central Europe to fell trees in winter, leave the top branches on and lay the tree on a slope with the top pointing downhill so that the remaining sap could drain from the tree.

Japanese priests chose cypress, a wood they considered sacred, for the construction of temples. The standing tree was ring-barked at different heights so that the sap could flow out and then felled several weeks later. Felling the tree was the ceremonial prelude to the eight years of intensive work that it took to complete the Ise Shrines. In Japan, as in the West, the precise moment of felling was determined by the position of the moon.

The time of year that a tree is felled has an important effect on the quality of the wood. A recent study of oak trees revealed that the chemical and physical properties of the wood change continually throughout the year. In February, oak contains the least amount of water, benzol ethanol and liquid carbohydrates. At that time, the wood has its greatest density and lowest rate of shrinkage. Even when stored, round stock goes through the same changes during the year and is therefore driest and easiest to work in February.

In some countries there are still laws in effect today that dictate when trees should be felled. One law stipulates that trees to be used in construction must be felled only in winter. Wood harvested in winter contains considerably less starch, which provides nourishment for all kinds of wood-destroying insects. It also has low moisture content, making it less likely to check and crack during the drying process.

The importance of cutting methods

The method of cutting determines how wood will later behave, both in terms of shrinkage and checking. Growth rings visible in the end grain should be short and of uniform length. This ideal situation can be attained by cutting four square timbers and one heartwood board from each log. If only two timbers are sawn from a log, they are more likely to check and twist along their length. Cutting one timber from a log reduces the amount of twisting, but the wood will still be prone to checking.

Flatsawn boards cut close to edge of the log are of poorer quality than quartersawn boards from the center. Too fast a feed rate when cutting a log will result in cracks on the surface of the wood. The best quality of cut is obtained by using a bandsaw mill, provided the machine is well maintained.

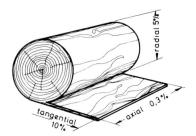

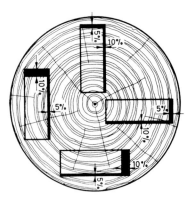

Top: Average wood shrinkage in three main directions. Above: Wood shrinks differently depending on where it is located in the log section. (Drawing by W. Nutsch)

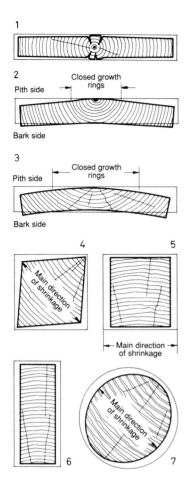

Shrinkage in cut wood.
(1) Quartersawn board from the center
of the log; (2) quartersawn board cut
through pith; (3) flatsawn board with
many growth rings cut on only one side;
(4) square timber with diagonal growth
rings; (5) square timber with parallel
growth rings; (6) quartersawn board
with parallel growth rings; (7) distortion
of round stock. (Drawing by W. Nutsch)

Drying and storing

Effective wood protection also depends on the methods used to dry and store cut lumber. Different rules apply for the carpenter and the cabinetmaker.

Although dendrochronological research has revealed that construction lumber has been worked green since the early Middle Ages, board stock must be dried before it can be used.

Construction lumber with a high moisture content is easiest for the carpenter to work. Timbers should be assembled soon after they have been dressed so that they do not twist and cause an inexact joint fit. Once the timbers have been assembled, good ventilation is necessary to allow them to dry. This is the only natural way to prevent the development of fungal spores, which discolor the wood and cause allergies in humans. Problems caused by blue-stain fungi have increased as trees have been weakened by acid rain, and today it is almost impossible to prevent discoloration in conifers by natural means.

Wood shrinkage can be used to advantage to create tight-fitting joints. A good example is provided in stairbuilding: If the stair stringers are greener than the treads, the treads will seat more tightly in their dadoed grooves as the stringers shrink. Conversely, incompatible wood joints lose their fit when the wood shrinks.

Board stock should be carefully stacked and left to season for several years, the specific amount of time depending on the species. Special rules apply for the storage of hardwoods that are susceptible to fungi, such as beech, maple, birch, apple and pear wood. If they are dried too fast, plum, acacia and root stock can split to such an extent that they are unusable. Wood containing tannin, such as oak, should be stored in the open for one to two years so that rain can wash away the acid.

Underwater storage is usually a good way to preserve and improve the quality of coniferous wood. Kiln-dried wood is of inferior quality to air-dried wood because artificial methods of drying create microscopic checks in the cell structure.

Structural wood protection

Structural wood protection encompasses all the measures taken to protect the structural members of a building from the destructive action of the weather. Some of the important elements that ensure effective wood protection include:
• Long roof overhangs, balconies, set-back facades, and gutters to protect facades from rain.
• Doors and windows recessed toward the inside and fitted with drip caps.
• Vertically installed siding with appropriate profiles and back ventilation. The bottom edge of the siding should be undercut with a bevel and stopped 30 cm. (1 ft.) above the ground to protect against splash.
• Glue joints on exterior doors cut at an angle, with the bevel sloping upward toward the inside.
• Undercut bevels on exposed end grain (which can also be covered to provide extra protection). The exposed ends of horizontal beams should be cut back at an angle, and on balconies, they should be capped, flashed or otherwise protected. The end grain on shutters should be protected with edge molding.
  Special rules apply for exposed exterior joinery. Joints should be constructed in such a way that no end grain is exposed. Horizontal corner joints should be chamfered so that no moisture can accumulate in the inside corner.
• The tenon on the lower end of a post should be offset toward the inside of the building and, if necessary, the bottom of the mortise should be drilled through so that any water can drain from the joint.
• The exposed upper edges of horizontal beams should be beveled toward the exterior. Exposed horizontal grooves that face upward should slope toward a low point where a hole is drilled to permit drainage.

- Beams passing through masonry should rest on an oak underlay.
- A gap of a few centimeters should be allowed where chimneys pass through openings in joists and rafters. This ventilation is necessary to prevent the formation of condensation as a result of differences in temperature between the brick wall and the wood beams. Exterior woodwork that is constantly exposed to the weather, such as cornice boards, barge boards, eaves and rafter tails, should be replaced as necessary.
- All exposed timbers should be planed and chamfered, since smooth surfaces dry faster than rough surfaces.

Chemical preservatives

Until 1832, the main chemical wood preservative used was wood vinegar, and in special cases, creosote. However, houses built with untreated wood survived just as well for hundreds of years.

It wasn't until wood was used for mine construction, railroad ties and electrical poles that the need to protect wood exposed to extreme stresses led to the widespread production and use of wood preservatives. Today, regulations in a number of countries require the use of preservatives on construction timbers that are indispensable for the stability of a building. Multitudes of wood preservatives are now available, almost all of them hazardous to health to a lesser or greater extent. Wood preservatives that contain salt, which are widely used, rapidly lose their effectiveness when treated timbers are exposed to the rain.

Chemical wood preservatives cannot be used as a substitute for good wood selection and appropriate measures of protection.

The Development of Wood Construction

We turn now to a brief discussion of the development of wood construction, at least to the extent that available sources permit. The oldest existing roof structure dates from about 1000 A.D. Various wooden building fragments that have survived from the 4th century provide us with information on earlier methods of construction. A basis for understanding even earlier structures can be found in art, in notched openings left in masonry where roof beams once rested, in stone imitations of wood constructions and in wood remnants preserved in water and bogs.

Japan's Ise Shrines are a particularly valuable source of information on bygone construction methods. Since the 7th century, these Shinto shrines have been carefully reconstructed every 20 years, always keeping to the original design.

Pole, post and palisade buildings

The earliest dwellings in Japan were hollows in the ground that were covered with a roof. The supporting stakes were sunk into the ground, a technique that was also used in European pole and post buildings. At about the same time, palisade structures were built in Europe, with walls constructed of vertical trunks set side by side in the ground.

Stave buildings

Stave construction, a refinement of post building, developed in northern and southern Europe during the 4th century. Wood columns up to 10 m. (33 ft.) long extended to the foot purlins and ridge purlin, making it possible to build purlin roof trusses with relatively large spans. These wood columns, which are found in the same form in Japanese temples, were possibly imitations of earlier stone architecture. Initially, the columns extended deep into the ground, which gave them their structural stability. This framework of columns was crowned by a rectangle of plates housed in open mortises cut in the upper ends of the corner posts, or staves. The intermediary column ends were housed in a groove in the plate. On the lower end, a sill was tenoned between the columns with a groove on its upper edge to receive the vertical wall planks. The bottom of the groove sloped downward, and at its deepest point a hole was drilled to permit drainage toward the outside. This method of construction was soon abandoned, presumably because it did not provide sufficient protection for the wood. Subsequently, the wall planks were placed on the exterior side of the sill, with a hook-shaped notch on the inside.

The introduction of the groundsill

The next stage in building development was to find a way to protect the buried ends of the columns from decay. The first attempts to set the columns on a continuous frame of sills can be traced back to about 1000 A.D. During the 11th century, a groundsill was introduced under the frame of sills. The groundsill itself was set on a carefully assembled mound of stones. In this way, the entire building was raised off the ground, and the columns, tenoned into the sill, were protected from decay. However, the stability of the building, which had previously been provided by the buried columns, was appreciably reduced.

The introduction of the groundsill triggered revolutionary change in building construction. New methods of construction had to be devised to solve the completely new problems of stability. For example, structural failure could result if the sills shifted significantly relative to each other. To provide the necessary stability, carpenters had to develop new techniques for making joints that were both resistant and fit with extreme precision.

Plated butt joints, laps, and mortise and tenons were some of the joints that came into use. Wall plates were trapezoid beams that were cogged over the projecting ends of the groundsill and joined at the corners with lap joints. The way the four corners were reinforced is particularly impressive. The columns' bases were mortised to slip over the corner lap joints on the plate beams and lock them in position (see the bottom drawing at right).

Chinese and Korean carpenters working in Japan and carpenters in the West came up with the same joinery solutions. Although there is no proof, it may well be that this was a result of an exchange of experiences along the Silk Road, an ancient trade route between the East and the West.

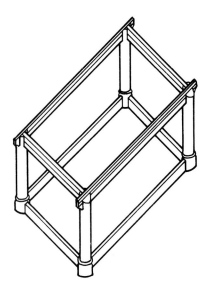

In frame construction, which was at its height during the 11th century, walls were enclosed in a solid frame. The walls were built of planks, wattle and daub, masonry, or other material. (Drawing by P. Pundt)

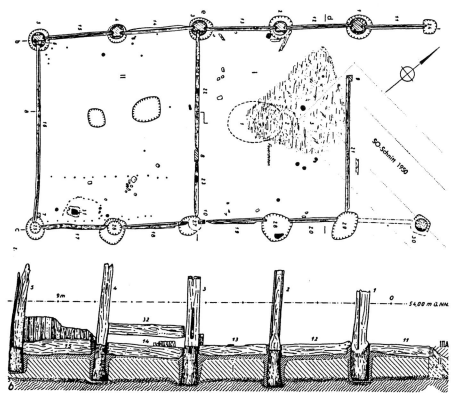

This drawing in plan and elevation of Motte Husterknupp, house 3, shows the well-preserved construction of a stave building with sill plates tenoned between the posts. (Drawing after A. Herrnbrodt, 1958)

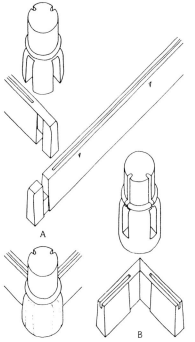

Corner sill joints on stave churches (Drawing by H. Christie)

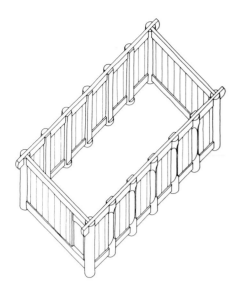

*Frame construction in sections,
Husterknupp, house 3
(Drawing after H. Christie, 1976)*

Timber-frame construction techniques

The original European stave-church construction with the columns anchored in the ground was, in itself, a logical way to build. But a number of structural problems arose when the columns were placed directly on a framework of sills. As a result, this method of construction was largely abandoned by the end of the 12th century, to be replaced by building methods whose basic principles have survived to the present.

In one type of frame construction, rigid wall panels were joined together (see the drawing at left). Elsewhere, bent frameworks were developed. In bent construction, bents were lined up behind each other and tied together by longitudinal beams; in this way it was possible to build wooden structures to any length. Each bent consists of a bottom plate, two principal posts, a top plate, roof posts and a pair of rafters. Log building, a third method of construction, evolved out of the need to use short logs when long construction timbers became scarce.

The widespread use of timber decreased its availability, and shortages gave rise to new construction methods. The Romanesque period witnessed, on the one hand, the development of stone and clay architecture and, on the other hand, methods of construction that required the use of bents at only every fourth or fifth rafter pair.

Some of these building traditions have survived through regional building practices. Timber-frame buildings with load-bearing plank walls are still common in Switzerland. Chalet building is nothing more than a refinement of log building. The raised posts on many farm buildings in Germany's Black Forest are reminiscent of the long wooden columns used in post buildings. Timber-frame construction is still very much alive today.

In bent construction, two upright wall posts are joined with a horizontal beam and a pair of rafters to form a bent. Lengthwise purlins tie the bents together. This method of construction predominated in Europe between the 8th and 11th centuries. (Drawing by P. Pundt)

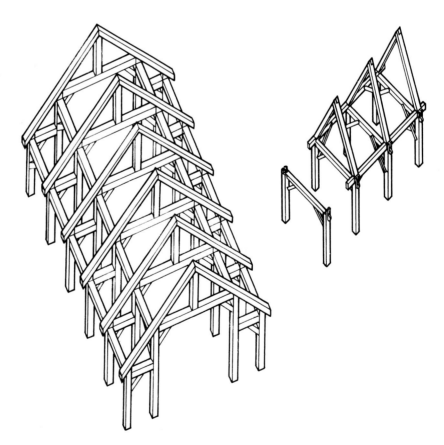

Traditional Roof Construction

Traditional roof construction can be divided into two main categories: purlin roofs and rafter roofs. They differ in the way that they transfer forces acting on the surface of the roof to the walls. The total load a roof places on its substructure is the weight of the building materials, intermediary floors and any snow. Wind exerts lateral pressure.

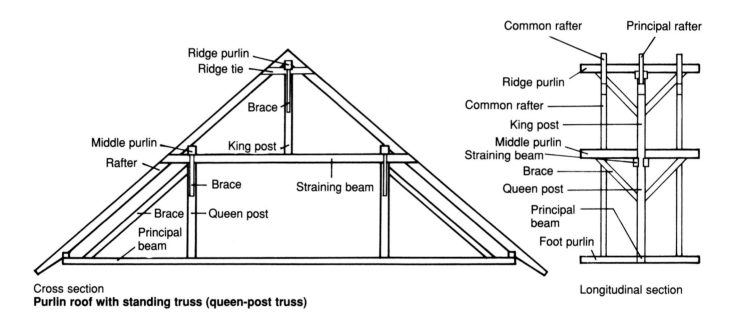

Cross section
Purlin roof with standing truss (queen-post truss)

Longitudinal section

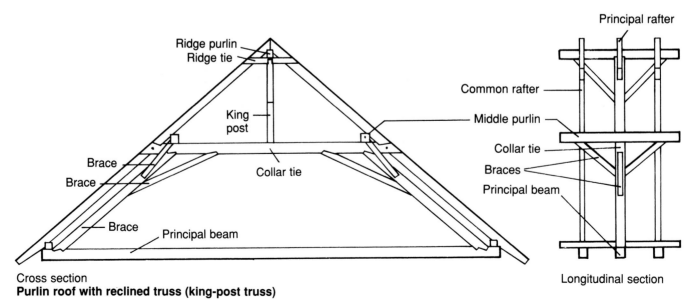

Cross section
Purlin roof with reclined truss (king-post truss)

Longitudinal section

Purlin roofs

Purlin roofs are the older of the two roof types. Rafters are supported by horizontal purlins that run along the length of the roof. In standing trusses (see the top drawing on the facing page), the purlins are borne by vertical wall, roof (queen) and ridge (king) posts. In Japanese houses, the purlins are supported by a framework of beams, which are often twisted. Depending on the size of the building, the roof will have a foot (bottom) purlin, one or more intermediate purlins and a ridge purlin. Collar ties between the middle purlins transfer horizontal loads. The rafter pair above the bent (the principal rafters) is connected with a collar tie. In older construction, braces parallel to the principal rafters dispersed the load on the principal beams and provided additional transverse stability. These braces form an immovable triangle that is resistant to lateral forces of compression. The longitudinal stability of the roof is provided by angle braces between the purlins and the posts.

To make better use of the space under the roof, so-called "reclined trusses" were invented. In this application, the queen posts are omitted and load is transferred to the principal beams by the braces alone. The thrust caused by the angled position of the braces is borne by the collar tie and the principal beam. Boards placed diagonally under the rafters ("wind braces") can be used instead of braces to give the roof longitudinal stability.

Post-supported purlin roofs

Traditional Japanese buildings usually have purlin roofs supported by short posts or stanchions. The rafters are hung in tension from the ridge pole and borne by post-supported middle purlins and foot purlins.

Post-supported purlin roof with arched, toothed collar beams (developed by Firma Hotzenholz, Herrischried, Germany)

Japanese post-supported purlin roof with spliced collar beam

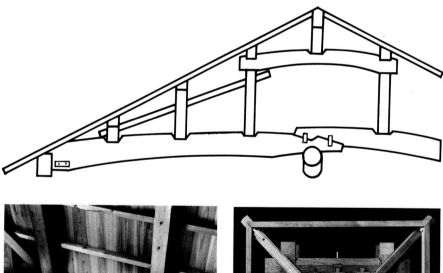

View from below, and above, of a Japanese roof truss with post-supported purlins

Rafter roofs

In the Middle Ages, rafter roofs were considered superior to purlin roofs. Since there are no intermediate posts, the rafters are self-bearing between the bottom of the rafter and the ridge. The compression force created by the slope of the rafters must be borne by the ceiling joists. On wide spans the rafters are supported by collar ties or cross (scissor) bracing.

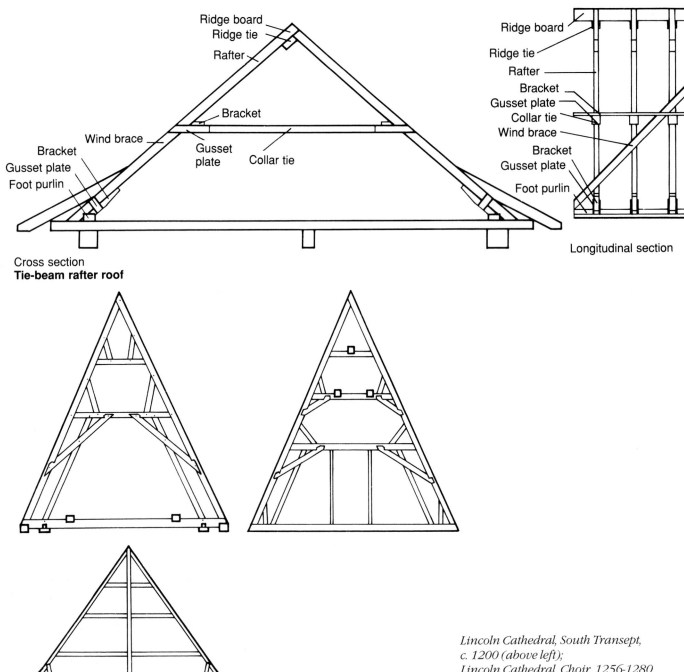

Cross section
Tie-beam rafter roof

Longitudinal section

Medieval roof construction (drawing by N. Fradgley and G. Wilson)

Lincoln Cathedral, South Transept, c. 1200 (above left);
Lincoln Cathedral, Choir, 1256-1280 (above right).
Church of Our Lady, Marburg, mid-13th century (left)

The best examples of cross-braced rafter roofs can be found in the great cathedrals that were built in England and Germany between the 13th and 15th centuries. As with purlin roofs, longitudinal rigidity was provided with the aid of wind braces under the rafters and a ridge pole. The collar ties often served as a framework for ceilings.

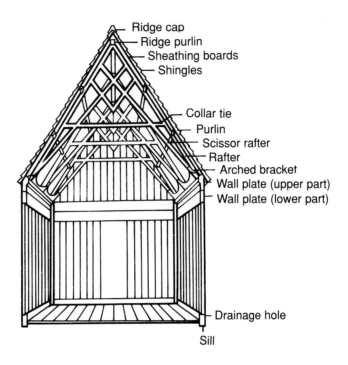

Construction elements in a stave-wall church

Traditional Chinese Wood Construction

The oldest known building code was introduced in China during the 12th century. The code was conceived out of a need to lower the high cost of public buildings. To this end, all buildings were divided into eight classes according to size, and for each size dimensions were fixed for the timbers required. In this way, the load-bearing capacity of each beam was determined in advance, and the material could be taken from stock. The code established that the ratio between the width and thickness of building timbers should be 2:3. Interestingly, the directives that appear in the code's building manual under the title "Ying-tsao-fa-shih" are a throwback to ancient methods of construction, as revealed by archaeological discoveries from the 5th century B.C.

Traditional Chinese construction is characterized by wooden columns resting on stone plinths, which in turn sit on a foundation of earth, gravel and broken brick. A later development was the addition of a wooden base plate between the end of the column and the stone plinth (see the drawing at right). This base plate, which was easily replaceable in case of decay, protected the ends of the columns. The exterior columns are tied into a sole plate that runs around the entire building and, at their upper ends, to a heavy top plate. The corner columns, which lean slightly inward, are tapered along their upper third and joined at their top end to a block that supports a complex system of brackets. The inclination of the columns increases the stability of the building, which is further strengthened by the addition of braces under the purlins and cross beams between the pillars.

The construction of the bracket complexes that carry the roof truss required particular care. Each bracket complex consists of blocks of various sizes, bracket arms and lever arms, which are interlocked with tenons and cog joints. Two of the five bracket arms are at right angles to the building's axis, the others are parallel with it. Each type of arm has a specific position in the bracket complex (see the drawings on the facing page) and a fixed cross-sectional dimension. The roof purlins rest on the uppermost arms. In the bracket complexes on top of the exterior columns, the eaves are carried by a bracket arm and an oblique lever arm in such a way that the weight of the roof, which is borne by the purlin, pushes one end of the lever arm down while the other end pushes the load of the eaves up.

A number of purlins carry thin rafters that extend only from one purlin to the next. The top end of each rafter is nailed to the purlin, while the lower end rests loosely on the purlin below. The rafters are sheathed, and tile is set into mortar over the sheathing.

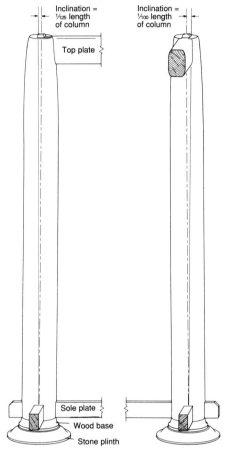

The columns of a traditional public building rest on wooden bases that themselves sit on a stone plinth. The columns are not anchored to the foundation. The stability of the exterior columns is provided by sole plates and top plates. These columns lean slightly inward: East-west oriented columns (along the building's length) deviate from plumb by 1/100 of total column length; north-south columns deviate 1/125 of column length. All wooden members are joined with housed mortise-and-tenon joints. The support block for the bracket complex rests on the top end of the column.

The wood used in traditional Chinese construction was white cedar, which is about four times more resistant to tension than steel and six times more resistant to compression than concrete. Buildings over a thousand years old attest to the effectiveness of this method of construction in providing protection against hurricanes and earthquakes, which are relatively frequent occurrences in China.

The roof structure is extremely flexible, because it is stiffened with a only few joints. The vibrations caused by earthquakes are absorbed by the friction of the wooden members, which though joined together can still move. A building's ability to sway a little prevents the buildup of resonance, because the building's vibrations are much slower than those of the earthquake.

The system of bracket complexes ensures the roof's horizontal rigidity. Because the columns are not anchored to the stone plinths, there is no risk of breakage at that point as a result of tension.

The weight of a traditional Chinese tiled roof is between 280 kg and 400 kg per sq. m. (57 lb. to 82 lb. per sq. ft.), compared to a modern European tile roof weighing about 100 kg per sq. m.(20 lb. per sq. ft.). This great roof load, in combination with the sweeping roof design, provides protection against hurricane-force storms.

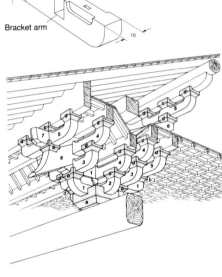

Bracket arm

In this bracket complex, which is typical of traditional Chinese construction, the large connecting block (a) rests on the top plate and supports the center bracket arm, or "flower" arm (1), and the cross arm (2). These arms carry the joint blocks (b) and small blocks (d) that support two oval arms (3). Above the oval arms are three long arms (4), one oblique lever arm (6) and three regular arms (5). The lever arm tapers to a "nose" on the bottom end and is held in place by three wedge-shaped members (7). The middle brackets (c) and the small brackets (d) on the two upper regular arms bear the beam for the eaves (at left in the drawing) and a purlin with a cleat under it (at right).

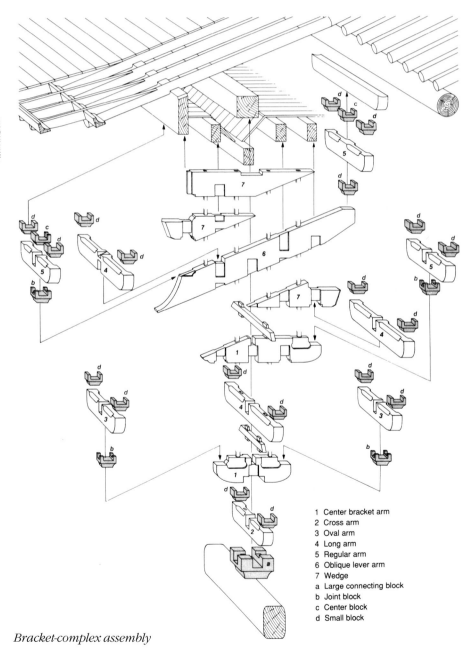

1 Center bracket arm
2 Cross arm
3 Oval arm
4 Long arm
5 Regular arm
6 Oblique lever arm
7 Wedge
a Large connecting block
b Joint block
c Center block
d Small block

Bracket-complex assembly

Joinery in Japanese Buildings

Professor Okawa, Kyoto

Wood joinery played a fundamental role in the development of Japanese construction techniques, which explains why there are so many different kinds of joints.

Methods of joinery vary, depending on the function and the age of the building. During the Edo period (1603-1868) more than 100 different joints were required for the construction of a single shrine or temple. Today, the roofs of ordinary Japanese houses are often built according to modern European construction methods, which means that metal fasteners are used extensively, and only about 20 joints are needed.

In modern Japanese temple building the diversity of joints has been maintained, and at least 100 different joints are still used. Appropriate joints are selected according to the type of wood, its cross section and its position in the building. A master carpenter must know approximately 200 joints, including variations that arise where two timbers cross at a right angle or obliquely.

The wood joints that originated at the dawn of Japanese architecture had an extraordinary diversity and refinement. However, during the Heian period (794-1185) the number of basic joints used in Buddhist temples declined, as did their quality. The joint forms in use at this time, such as *art* (dovetails), *kama* gooseneck joints), *hozo* (simple mortise and tenon) and *watariago* (cogged joints), were probably introduced into Japan from China and Korea with Buddhist architecture.

At the beginning of the Kamakura period (1185-1336), when the first Japanese building guilds were established, the development of wood joints took a great leap forward. The craftsmen of the period began to work independently, taking on the functions of architects and passing on their experience to their offspring. By contrast, during the earlier Heian Period, workers constructed all buildings under the direction of a small bureaucracy of architects.

Once the guilds were organized, innovation in joinery rested solely in the hands of the carpenter. Joint design was adapted to new methods of construction. Craftsmen introduced new methods of joinery adapted to the *Shoin-zukuri* style of domestic architecture (15th to 16th century), with its multitude of *toko* (alcoves) and *tana* (shelving), and to the *Hikari-zuke* teahouse style (16th to 17th century).

Ancient Japanese dwelling of natural hinoki *wood. No nails are used in the structure, only wedges and mortise-and-tenon joints.*

A special corner joint was devised to tie pillars and beams of round stock. As well as being adapted stylistically to the new methods of construction, this joint was better able to resist forces of tension and compression and, at the same time, it prevented structural timbers from shifting and twisting. To overcome the technical difficulties, new, complicated mortise-and-tenon joints *(hozo)* with wooden keys *(sen)* were introduced. These joints could resist forces in all directions, and, in addition, they were aesthetically pleasing.

In Japan, beauty is an integral part of wooden joinery. In early Japanese joinery, the end grain of tenons and keys was often exposed. Examples can be found in ancient temples and in old farmhouses. In such cases, it is easy to see how the joint was made. But as joinery evolved, tenons and keys were more often concealed. For example, if two square timbers are joined at a right angle at a corner of a building, all that is visible is the side of the triangle and the 45° miter on the top surface. What is within the joint is not obvious. Similarly, when a beam is tenoned into an an upright, the treenail used to pin the tenon is usually concealed behind the wall covering.

As joinery became more and more refined, some joints appeared that owed more to the art of puzzle making than to technical necessity or aesthetic value. In addition, a number of edge joints were devised with complex decorative curves, but they were seldom used.

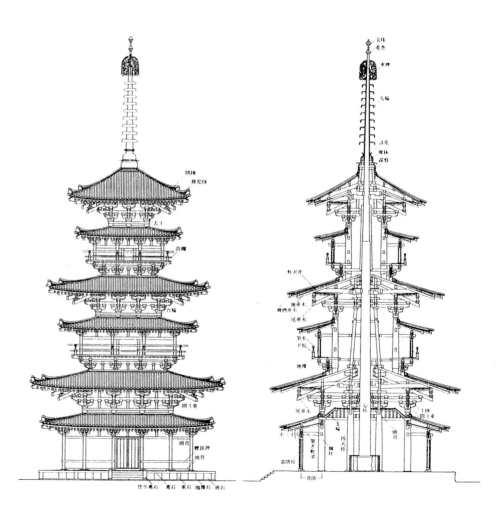

Front view and cross section of the Yakuski Pagoda in Japan, erected in 730 A.D. according to traditional Chinese building methods

It is not by mere chance that so many ingenious joints have evolved in Japanese architecture. In a country like Japan, which is subjected to violent typhoons and earthquakes, it was advantageous to use timbers for posts and beams that were as long as possible. This method of construction with numerous junctions between posts and beams required a multitude of cross joints and corner joints. If a foot purlin was spliced along its length because a long timber was not available, the joints had to have approximately the same load-carrying capacity as a continuous beam.

The wood used in traditional Japanese architecture, especially *hinoki* wood (Japanese cypress), was usually highly resistant yet easy to work with. Using European softwood for certain Japanese joints would make these joints considerably more difficult to cut and construct.

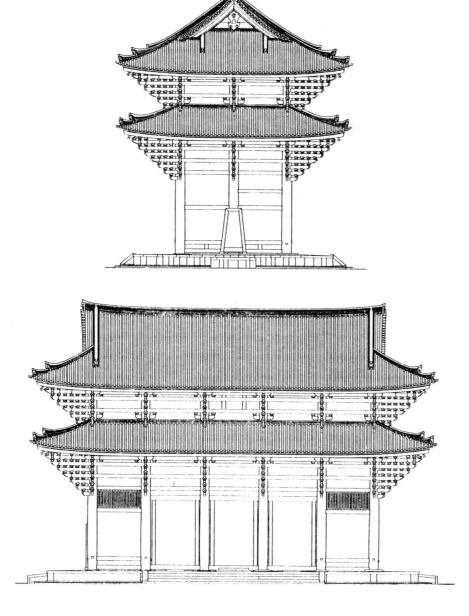

Gable view and side view of Japan's Todai Temple, dating from 1191

It is also important to mention the traditional forms of expression unique to Japanese architecture. An example is the temple-and-shrine architecture with its projecting roof overhangs at the eaves and curved roof lines. From the front, it often appears that there are only right-angled cuts, but a three-dimensional view reveals that the parts of the joint do not cross at right angles. In this way, angled joinery becomes more complex. Japanese interiors with built-in furnishings, such as *toko* or *chigaitana* (stepped shelving), require other visible joints.

The Japanese have a discerning eye for wood with beautiful color, and construction timbers with uniform grain are highly prized. Visible through mortise and tenons and visible pegs and keys are avoided where possible, because exposed end grain *(koguchi)* is considered unsightly.

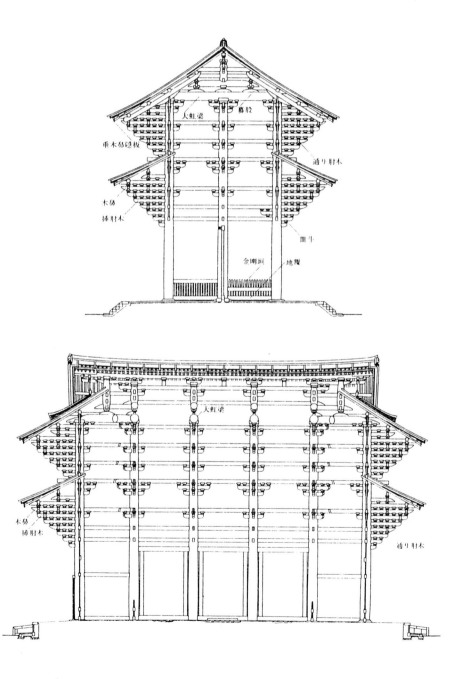

The cross sections show the projecting bracket complexes, which were introduced to Japan by Buddhist temple builders from China.

Joint Forms

Wood joinery is the mating of two or more surfaces to form a solid unit that serves a specific purpose. In the following presentation, the different types of joints are not categorized according to application. Instead, a number of basic forms are introduced—in the case of splicing joints, the butt, lapped scarf, mortise and tenon, and dovetail joint—and then the various combinations of these forms that are used in wood construction and cabinetmaking are examined.

It is impossible to appreciate the complex forms of eastern and western wood joints without a thorough understanding of the basic forms. Once fundamental joinery has been mastered, new types of joints can be developed and refined as circumstances dictate.

The easiest way to enhance your understanding of each joint form is to let your hands be your guide. Re-creating existing joint designs is the key to discovering what was in the minds of the craftsmen who invented them.

To choose the most appropriate joint for a building or piece of furniture, it is important to consider carefully the different forces acting on the structure. The characteristics of the wood used should also be taken into account, as should the part of the tree from which the wood was cut.

Making a joint on the wrong end of a timber can easily result in splitting and, ultimately, failure of the joint. The only way to develop an "eye" for the irregularities hidden beneath the wood's surface is to spend a lot of time working with wood.

The joints used by cabinetmakers and those used by carpenters are not treated separately, since the logic of these joints is the same. Considering the joints together provides a clearer overview than would otherwise be possible. Joints that serve purely artistic or ornamental purposes are not covered in this book.

Depending on the position of the mating timbers, joints must be made both with the grain and across the grain. With this in mind, the joints are presented in the following order:

1. Splicing joints for lengthening horizontal and vertical timbers.

2. Oblique joints for joining timbers at angles less than 90°.

3. Corner joints for connecting timbers at right angles.

4. Edge joints for joining boards edge to edge.

1 Splicing Joints

Splicing joints, or scarf joints, are used in the following applications:

1. They are used to lengthen posts, which can often extend through several stories in Japanese wood construction. This method was developed to make it possible to replace the lower ends of the huge, round columns used in temple architecture, which were particularly prone to decay. Posts and columns were fitted with so-called "root joints," which could be taken apart to allow easy replacement of the bases.

2. Long timbers for beams and girders are difficult to erect in full length. Thus it is often necessary to fabricate horizontal timbers in sections and assemble them as the structure is erected. These sectional timbers are particularly important in Japanese buildings, because diagonal cross bracing was not used in traditional Japanese architecture. The necessary rigidity was obtained instead by joining several horizontal members to the posts to resist the forces of tension and compression.

The soundness of traditional building methods has actually been forgotten in Japan. Under present-day building codes, builders cannot get credit from a bank unless they incorporate bracing in the walls, under the false assumption that this will add to the stability of the building. In reality, braces are unnecessary because the cross beams and posts provide the necessary rigidity. And in the event of an earthquake, structural braces can cause the joints of a building to pop open because they negate its flexibility. In addition, cross bracing makes it difficult to make openings in walls.

3. Splicing joints are used whenever the natural length of a timber is shorter than that needed for horizontal members, such as beams, sills, purlins, girts and joists. They are also used to extend the length of rafters.

4. Because framing beams for exposed balconies are vulnerable to decay, the beams must be replaceable. Splicing joints are used at the point where projecting beams pass through the exterior wall of the building.

5. Splicing joints are used by cabinetmakers when stock of the required length is not available. They are also used to repair individual boards.

In addition to the structural considerations outlined here, certain historical conditions have also favored the development and dissemination of splicing joints. The expansion of building activity in the early Middle Ages and the use of construction methods that required large quantities of timber led to a shortage of wood suitable for construction, both in Japan and Europe. Even in regions that had previously been heavily forested, it became increasingly difficult to find trees of suitable size and regular growth, especially in Europe, where forestry was a privilege reserved for the nobility.

Log construction, which began in the Middle Ages, required the use of small-diameter timbers. Often, the necessary length could be obtained only by splicing together suitable sections from short trees. It wasn't until the 13th century that construction methods were developed that made it possible to use shorter, bowed timbers, and to use far fewer structural timbers to provide the necessary rigidity.

In Japan, the problem of the shortage of straight timbers was overcome more by refining splicing joints than by developing new building techniques.

Joint Construction

For all joints, it is essential to make the mate that will carry the greatest load on the upper end of the wood. The upper end, which can be identified by the orientation of the growth rings in both round timber and beams, is the part that grew toward the top of the tree. The difference in quality between the two ends is caused by the pyramid-like growth of the annual rings that continually overlap each other along the tree's length.

When making splicing joints, it is advisable to join upper ends to each other. The foot ends are more likely to split, because grain direction is oriented toward the outside. Similarly, an oblique grain direction, caused by irregular growth as in reaction wood, will also impair the stability of a joint, because cuts that are not perpendicular to the grain tend to tear out. Joining the correct ends is especially important for joints that are subject to forces of tension and for dovetails and miters across the grain.

The traditional guidelines for the construction of Japanese Ise shrines even stipulated the correct orientation of the timbers. For example, the timber for the lintel above an entrance should have its upper end toward the right, as seen from the outside. For joints on the interior that carry lighter loads, timbers should be joined foot end to foot end to create an aesthetically pleasing grain figure.

For the most part, even for complicated joinery, the Japanese try not to leave any joint lines visible, except for angled cuts that blend in with the grain better than right-angled cuts. In this way, craftsmanship is hidden beneath the surface.

Similar tendencies are also apparent in the West. In southern Austria, for example, the main construction joints of a house were considered as good spirits and were hidden with wood paneling. And in Germany after World War II, debris in bombed churches revealed that stone masons had concealed elaborate stone figurines in several stone columns.

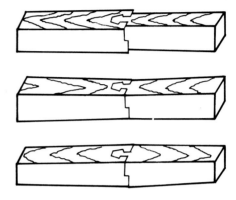

Splicing joints

Top: Foot end mated to upper end, with the male part on the upper end (Okuri-tsugi).
Middle: Upper end to upper end —the most stable joint (Ikiai-tsugi).
Bottom: Foot end to foot end —this joint, which produces an aesthetically pleasing figure, should be used only on timbers that carry light loads and should not be wedged (Wakare-tsugi).

Butt Joints

The joint forms with which we begin are not joints in the true sense of the word. To apply them in practice, they must be combined with other joints or fasteners. However, to understand the development of joinery, it is important to examine its basic forms.

The easiest way to join two beams lengthwise is to make a square cut at the end of each beam and mate the two ends together. Obviously, a joint of this kind must be supported in some way, either by a beam, a masonry wall or by some other flat, solid surface. Because the ends are not connected, they can pull away from each other at any time. Beams joined in this way can only carry compression loads across their horizontal plane, and there is a danger that heavy loads will cause the joint to fail, especially if the beam ends rest on a narrow support.

The **butt joint** is a commonly used joint that, in practice, is always secured with a key or wedge across the ends of the two mating parts. Gluing a butt joint is effective only if the pores on the end-grain surfaces are first filled with a thinned adhesive.

Adhesives are of limited importance for the carpenter, because woods used in construction are usually too wet to allow gluing. In addition, the quick drying time of adhesives is not suited to the demands of house construction, and it not possible to achieve the precision required for good glue joints when working with squared timbers.

Adhesives play a more important role in cabinetmaking, though they do not replace the use of appropriate joints. Adhesives can prevent simple joints from failing through slippage. Increasing a joint's surface area can make gluing more effective. One way to do this is to use an **offset butt joint,** though this joint still has to be secured with a key, pin or nails.

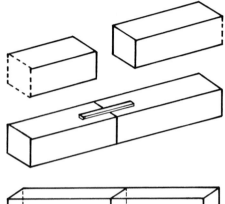

Simple butt joint

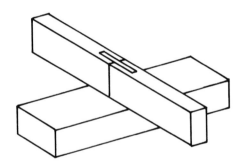

Butt joint fastened with a key

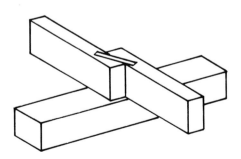

Offset butt joint fastened with a key

Splayed Joints

Splayed joints and offset splayed joints are similar to butt joints, but the area of their mating surfaces is greatly increased by angling the cuts. This provides a better gluing surface, which makes splayed joints of much greater importance than butt joints for cabinetmakers.

Splayed scarf joints are useful for lengthening structural timbers such as rafters, though they still require nailing. A splayed scarf joint suitable for splicing rafters is shown in the middle drawing at right.

Tapered finger joints, which are made by machine, extend the principle of the splayed joint. The greatly increased area of the mating surfaces makes these exceptional glue joints.

The halved splayed scarf (shown in the photo below) is a Japanese refinement of the simple splayed joint.

Although this joint is more difficult to cut, it is a very good glue joint, it provides effective protection against twisting as the wood expands and contracts, and it also prevents lateral movement.

The bird's mouth, or V-joint, can withstand stress from all directions, except along its length. In this direction, compression can cause the female end to split, and tension can cause the joint to separate. This type of joint is particularly suitable for floor framing, because it prevents beams from twisting. Diagonal halved scarf joints are also used in interior work.

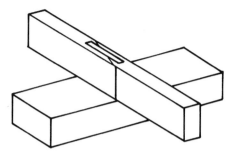

Simple splayed joint

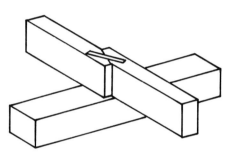

Offset splayed joint

Splayed scarf joint (Sogi-tsugi)

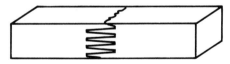

Tapered finger joint

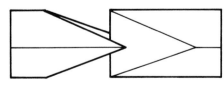

Bird's mouth or V-joint
(Ken-isuka-tsugi)

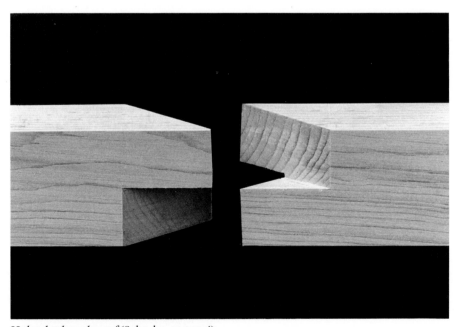

Halved splayed scarf (Saba-ko-sa-tsugi)

Lapped Scarf Joints

Lapped scarf joints are made with mating members that are cut to half thickness at their ends. The **straight half lap,** the simplest form, has three mating surfaces (compared with the butt joint's one). Lap joints can be cut in various ways to enable them to withstand different kinds of stress. They can withstand forces of compression and help to prevent vertical shifting. However, because half the thickness of the mating members is removed to make the joint, the wood is weakened in cross section. As a result, lap joints can be used only where vertical loads on the joint are insignificant or where they are adequately supported from below, as is the case with sills and purlins supported by a wall or horizontal beams stacked on top of each other in a log structure. If they are long enough, lap joints can be reinforced with wooden pegs to resist lateral stress.

In a **half-lapped V-joint,** the butt ends are cut at an angle, sometimes called a bird's mouth, which increases the contact area of the mating parts. The design of the joint enables it to withstand greater forces of compression longitudinally, because the angled butt ends cannot slide sideways so easily.

The **undercut half-lapped V-joint** provides even greater stability against lateral movement. If secured with screws or bolts, it can be used as a splicing joint for vertical posts.

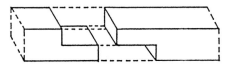

Straight half lap

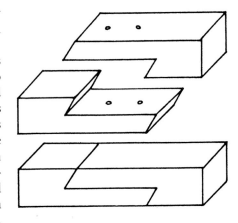

Half lap with splayed shoulders

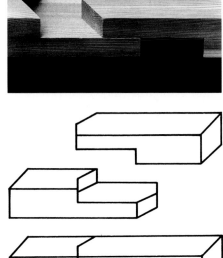

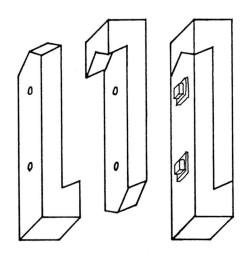

Half-lapped V-joint

Undercut half-lapped V-joint

Cutting the middle mating surfaces at an angle creates the **beveled half lap,** or compression joint. If a load is exerted from above, this joint locks together and prevents pullout.

If the method of construction does not allow a joint to seat through pressure, a wedge or key can be used to reinforce the joint, as in the **wedged half-lapped V-joint**.

Halved splayed joints

In Japan, it is also common to use the **keyed halved splayed joint** to prevent pullout. Known as the "stork's bill," this joint can be further reinforced by cutting the mating surfaces

at an oblique angle, which makes possible a number of variations:

mating surfaces slanting outward;
mating surfaces slanting inward;
cutting a tongue and groove;
adding a stub tenon.

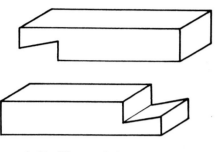

Beveled half lap (Arikaki-tsugi)

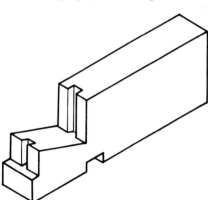

Beveled half lap with stub tenons

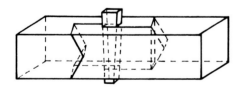

Wedged half-lapped V-joint

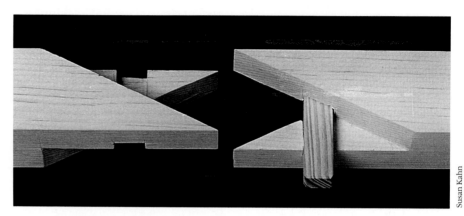

Susan Kahn

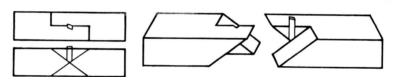

Keyed halved splayed joint (Isuka-tsugi)

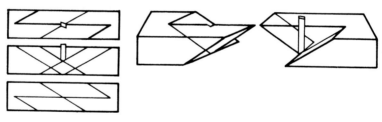

Keyed halved splayed joint with oblique mating surfaces (Miyajima-tsugi)

The oblique mating surfaces of wedged and pinned joints should not be too steep, or the wedge will be too close to the outer edge of the beam and the joint will be weakened.

Making these kinds of joints demands a high degree of creative ability and a sound knowledge of spatial geometry. The isometric drawing of the **halved splayed joint with tongue and groove** shown at right gives an idea of what is involved.

These types of joints are used in Japan when the construction is visible from three sides.

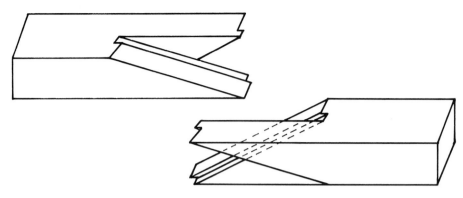

Halved splayed joint with tongue and groove

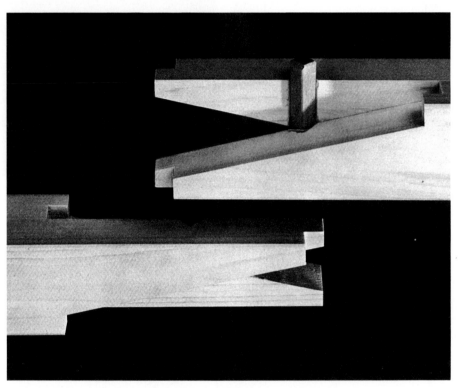

Diagonally keyed halved splayed joint with stub tenons (Sumikiri-isuka-tsugi)

Mortise-and-Tenon Joints

Whereas the lap joint prevents vertical movement, the **mortise and tenon** secures the mating parts so that they do not move laterally. The joint also prevents twist and retains its precision fit as the wood shrinks.

Combining the mortise and tenon and the half lap creates the **lapped mortise and tenon.** This joint stabilizes its members against both lateral and vertical shifting, thereby eliminating the possibility of twist. Because lapped mortise-and-tenon joints are easy to make, they are often used on sills and on purlins that are supported by posts. Using wooden fishplates or metal fishplates, bolted and sometimes mortised into the sides of these joints, provides the necessary resistance against tension. Under heavy loads, the lapped mortise and tenon should also be supported by a hardwood cleat.

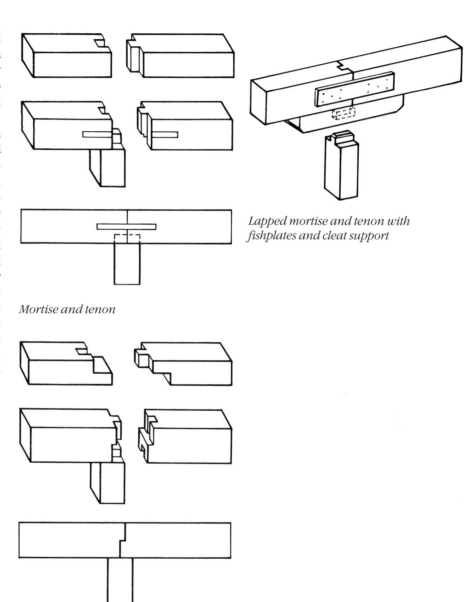

Lapped mortise and tenon with fishplates and cleat support

Mortise and tenon

Lapped mortise and tenon

Rod mortise and tenons

In Japanese construction, posts that run from the groundsill to the top plate through several stories play a major role in ensuring the structural rigidity of a building. This explains the frequent use and perfection of a complex joint that is used to extend timbers. In literal translation, this joint is called a **lapped rod mortise and tenon.** It constitutes a development of the lapped mortise and tenon.

The tenons, which are weak because of their narrow cross section, are haunched to increase their load-bearing capacity. The strength of these joints lies in their resistance to pullout and twist. As long as the fit of the mating parts is exact, the weakening of the mortised upright is insignificant, because the outer zones of tension remain and the cut-out inner zones are filled with forces of compression.

Wedging these joints can make them even more secure. If an upright post is mortised to cross beams in only three directions, the third beam must be wedged or pegged to prevent pullout. An important application of this joint is in timber-frame construction where girders in longitudinal and transverse walls meet at a common post at the same height (see pp. 48-49). In the West, builders use metal fasteners at such junctions rather than cutting these intricate joints.

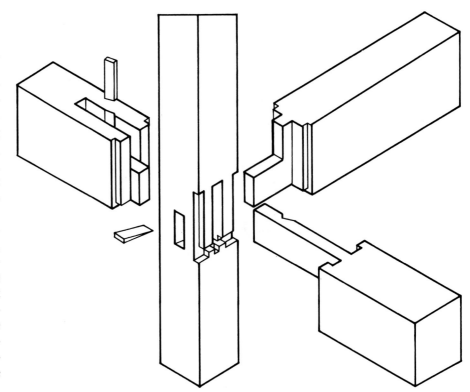

Through lapped rod mortise and tenon, wedged and haunched (Shi-ho-shachi-kumi-te)

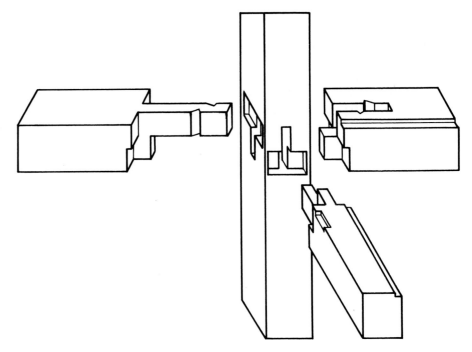

Through lapped rod mortise and tenon with diagonal keys (Sampo-zashi)

36

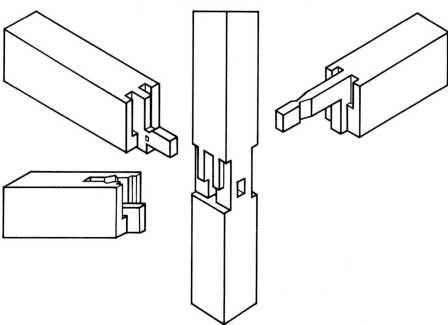

Junction of three or four cross beams and an upright post at the same height
(Saobiki-dokko)

The **rod mortise and tenon** can also be used to join just two beams to opposite sides of a post. In this application, the tenon's throat must be thicker in section.

The rod mortise and tenon is also used as a simple splicing joint on square or round timbers where increased length is required. For joints on supported beams or sills, two rabbeted slots for keys are used instead of a lap. This measure distributes compression load and prevents twist. Another application for the rod mortise and tenon joint is to lengthen projecting support beams for balconies (as discussed on p. 28).

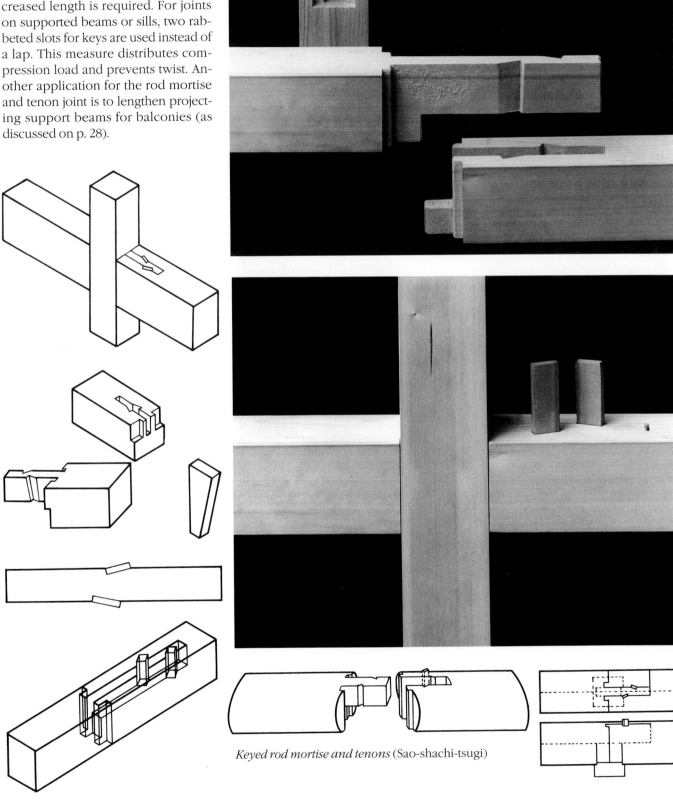

Keyed rod mortise and tenons (Sao-shachi-tsugi)

Slot mortise and tenons

Slot mortise-and-tenon joints used for splicing are known in both the West and the East. Except for the bolted bird's-mouth mortise and tenon, the examples in the drawings on this page are taken from furniture construction and are suitable for joining boards of narrow thickness. The stability of the joint is maintained by using wooden dowels or pegs.

The **slot mortise and tenon with undercut shoulders** is a good glue joint. The end-grain bevels increase the mating-surface area and prevent the mortise from opening.

The **double-tenon joint** is suitable for joining large-dimension frame members.

If a length of wood is too short to allow a tenon to be cut, a cross-grain **loose tenon** can be inserted into the mortises at the end of the two mating boards. The loose tenon should not be too thin. One advantage is that the mating parts are identically cut.

Offset double tenons can be used to join thin furniture-frame members through cross pieces. The same joint can also be made with a loose tenon.

The **upright mortise and tenon,** also known as the scissors joint, and the **bird's-mouth mortise and tenon** are suitable for joining large structural timbers. The mating members of these joints are bolted together.

Slot mortise and tenon

Slot mortise and tenon with undercut shoulders

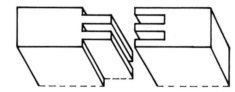

Double tenon joint

Loose tenon joint

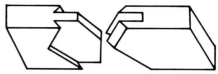

Bird's-mouth slot mortise and tenon with beveled shoulders

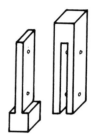

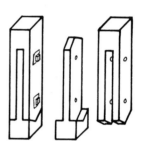

Upright mortise and tenon and bird's-mouth mortise and tenon, with bolts

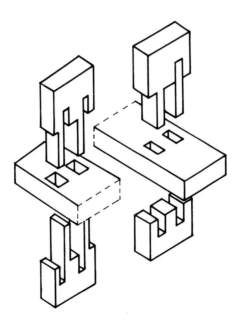

Offset through double tenons

Stub tenons

Stub tenons for longitudinal joinery come in a wide variety of designs. The **offset stub tenon** should always be shorter than the mating mortise, so that the end grain of the tenon does not bear all the compression load.

The wood used for these joints should be reasonably dry, so that the joint does not work loose as the wood shrinks. Using dry wood also protects against twist and splitting.

Crossed tenons provide the best protection against distortion, but their mortises fail easily when subjected to lateral pressure.

Unlike the offset tenon, the crossed tenon should be the same depth as the mortise that receives it. With this joint, the end-grain surface of the tenon is large enough to bear the compression load. Crossed tenons are sometimes reinforced with wooden plates.

A dowel can be used in place of the tenon, but the joint provides no resistance against twisting or breakage.

Half-blind stub tenon (Kakushi-mechigai-tsugi)

Half-blind L-shaped stub tenon (Kaneon-mechigai-tsugi)

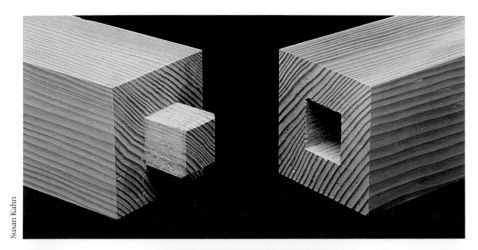

Square and fan-shaped stub tenons (Kakuhozo-imo-tsugi *and* Oagihozo-imo-tsugi)

Crossed stub tenon (Jyu-mon-ji-tsugi-te)

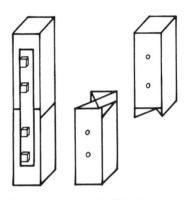

Ornamental crossed tenon

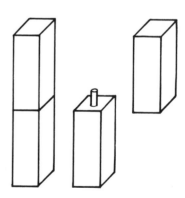

Crossed tenon with fishplates

A dowel in place of a tenon

Dovetail Joints

Cutting a dovetail on a tenon makes pullout of the joint impossible. Although dovetail joints are weak in tension because of short grain at the edges of the tails, careful wood selection can reduce the risk of shear failure. Particular attention should be given to the following:

1. Only straight-grained wood should be used for dovetail joints.

2. The tail (or female half) should always be cut on the wood's upper end.

3. The growth rings in the two mating pieces should be parallel in cross section, so that the different rates of shrinkage in a beam's thickness and width (radial and tangential shrinkage) do not result in an imprecise fit.

4. As far as possible, only dry wood should be used.

The simple **through dovetail,** which can resist pullout only along its length, is used mainly as a splicing joint on groundsills.

The **lapped dovetail** is a refinement of the through dovetail and provides additional protection against vertical shifting. However, this joint offers little resistance to bowing and twisting, because the dovetail's mating surfaces are very small. In Japan, dovetails are made a little shorter than in the West.

Adding a stub tenon to the lapped dovetail joint greatly improves its resistance to twisting. This joint was devised by Japanese and European carpenters for lengthening sill timbers and roof purlins in light timber-frame construction.

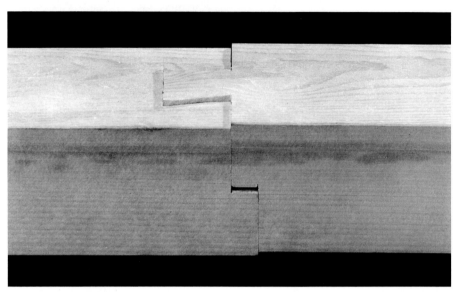

Lapped dovetail joint (Koshikake-ari-tsugi-te)

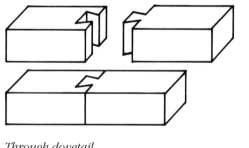

Through dovetail

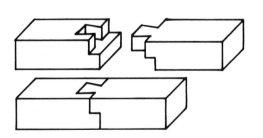

Lapped dovetail with half-blind stub tenon (Koshi-ire-mechigai-zuki-ari-tsugi)

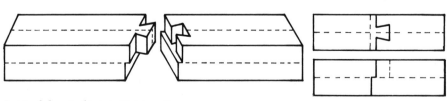

Lapped dovetail joints (Ari-tsugi)

Double dovetails

The **double dovetail joint** is a logical development of the lapped dovetail. The double dovetail has the same surface area on the sides of its mating tails as the simple through dovetail and therefore provides the same resistance to horizontal movement. But because the joint is lapped, it also protects against vertical movement.

The **double lapped dovetail,** which originated in Japan, represents a transitional stage between the lap joints and the tabled lap joints that will be described later. This joint is also sometimes called a **tabled lap joint with two dovetails**.

Symmetrical joinery is one of the characteristics of Japanese wood construction. The identical mating parts can be marked out together, which makes it considerably easier to construct the joint and ensures a precise fit. It's important to make sure that all the saw cuts are made on the waste side of the scribe lines. Otherwise, you'll end up with a joint line that is the thickness of the sawblade.

Cabinetmakers use double dovetail joints as decorative elements; carpenters use them where joints under tension are unsupported from below.

Double lapped dovetail (Ni-mai-ari-tsugi)

Double dovetail joint

Double lapped dovetail (Ryo-men-ari-tsugi)

Gooseneck joints

The gooseneck mortise-and-tenon joint, which is similar in principle to the dovetail joint, was devised to resist tension force. Different forms of this joint were in use in Japan as early as 1000 A. D.

The joint's male half has an extended tenon with a head that looks like a reversed dovetail. The weak point of the gooseneck joint is the mortise, which can split open wide enough as the wood shrinks to release the tenon from its housing. If one of the mating beams twists, the joint can easily come apart.

The **simple gooseneck joint** was commonly used in Japan during the Heian Period (794–1185). Improvements in tools made during the Edo Period (1603–1868) made it possible to refine the joint by adding rabbeted slots, which reduced the risk of twisting and pullout. The raised neck increased resistance to deflection. The same result is achieved today by employing a small stub tenon.

In modern Japanese wood construction, the various forms of the gooseneck joint are often designed to be self-supporting (that is, without support from a beam below). The mortise is made in the beam that bears the load and the tenon in the connecting timber. The length of the tenon should be double the width of the timber, but no more than 12 cm (4¾ in.) since additional length does not increase the load-bearing capacity.

Gooseneck joints are now made by machine in Japan, where they are greatly prized for their many and diverse uses.

The **mitered gooseneck joint,** which is particularly well suited to exposed joints because the miter cut blends inconspicuously with the grain, is used for exterior and interior cornices.

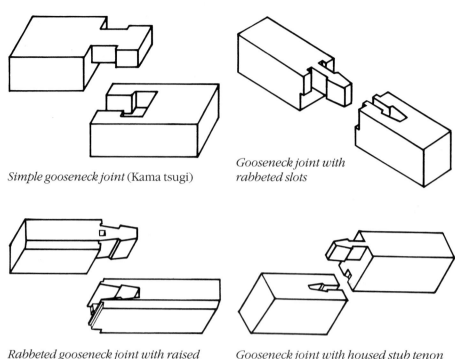

Simple gooseneck joint (Kama tsugi)

Gooseneck joint with rabbeted slots

Rabbeted gooseneck joint with raised neck

Gooseneck joint with housed stub tenon

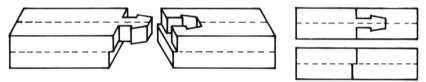

Lapped gooseneck joint

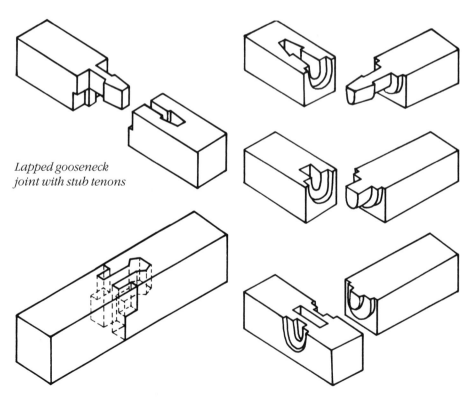

Lapped gooseneck joint with stub tenons

Old-style gooseneck joint with greater capacity to resist lateral force

Machine-made gooseneck joints

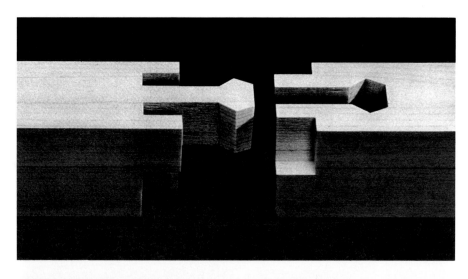

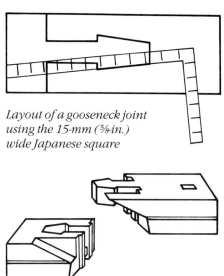

Layout of a gooseneck joint using the 15-mm (⅝-in.) wide Japanese square

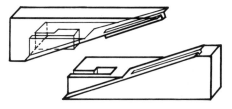

A decorative form of the joint, with half gooseneck and tongue and groove concealed in a splayed scarf

Lapped gooseneck joints with stub tenons (Noge-tsugi)

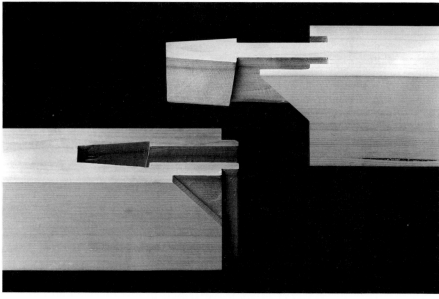

Mitered gooseneck joint (Koshikake-kama-tsugi)

Loose tenons and keys

One of the disadvantages of the rod mortise and tenon joints discussed on pp. 36-38 is that the extended tenons effectively shorten the length of construction beams. This can mean a loss of up to 12 cm (4¾ in.) on each tenoned beam.

One way to save wood is to insert a separate piece of wood into the mortises cut on the ends of the mating members. The key inserts should be made of hardwood that is drier than the wood that will house them. Joints made with loose tenons or keys can be used only on horizontal beams, and they must be supported from below.

Pinned loose rod tenons are especially useful on beams that must be joined at points where access is difficult. **Butterfly keys** are suitable for use in joints that may have to be taken apart from time to time, such as on modular cabinets.

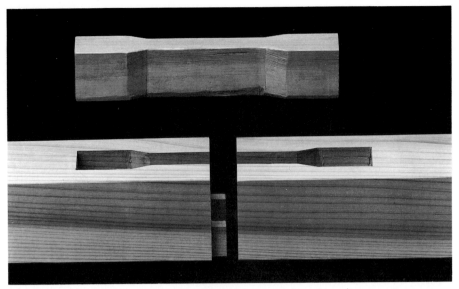

Butt joint with loose gooseneck tenon and stub tenons (Ryo-kine-gata-tsugi)

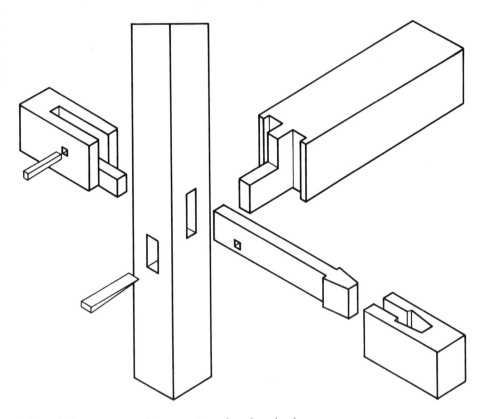

Through, loose gooseneck tenon, pinned and wedged

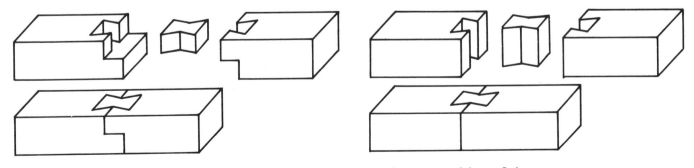

Half-lapped butt joint with butterfly key (Chigiri-tsugi-ari-kata) *and plain butt joint with butterfly key*

Four-way joints

Self-supporting columns and posts play an important role in traditional Japanese wood construction. Because the bases of these columns are particularly susceptible to rot, "root joints" were developed that made it possible to replace the rotted bases. The fact that these joints were four-way, that is, visible from all sides, encouraged Japanese carpenters to make the joint lines as inconspicuous as possible and to conceal the internal structure of the joint.

The **double gooseneck joint** is tapered and slipped into place diagonally. The **double dovetail joint** is made in the same way, but it opens only in one direction.

Entrance posts have a special significance in Japanese temple building. When Ise shrines are dismantled, which they usually are every 20 years, the wood is either burned or reused for other purposes. Only the two entrance columns are saved for use in a new temple or other sacred building.

Double gooseneck joint cut diagonally (Shi-ho-kama-tsugi-te)

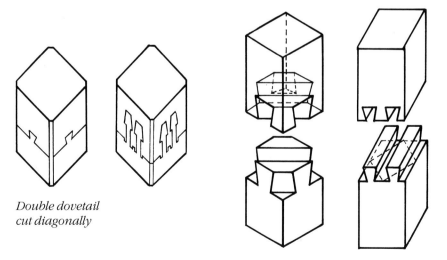

Double dovetail cut diagonally

The double dovetail and the double gooseneck joint are similar in construction.

The **self-aligning dovetail joints** shown in the drawings below were used on the main-entrance columns of Osaka Castle. Even today, it is necessary to replace the column bases from time to time. X-rays reveal whether the joint is opening from below.

These interlocking joints are wonders of craftsmanship. If they are made with a high degree of perfection, they are impossible to detect, but not to take apart.

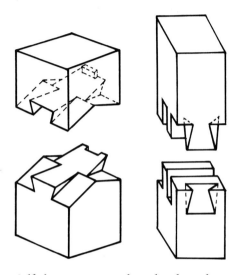

Self-aligning joint with wedge-shaped double dovetails

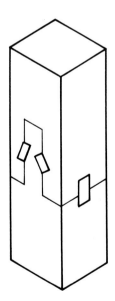

Keyed haunched mortise and tenon joint (Shachi-tsugi)

Rod mortise-and-tenon joints for timber framing

Japanese carpenters have developed unique ways of joining horizontal beams to vertical posts in timber-frame structures. Unknown in this form in the West, these tension-resistant joints provide rigidity for the partition walls without sacrificing the flexibility that is necessary to withstand earthquakes. By contrast, the diagonal corner bracing used in Western timber-frame construction breaks at its joints if subject to distortion.

In Japanese wood construction, a distinction is made between joints that connect elements with the same function (for example, beam with beam, or brace with brace) and joints that connect dissimilar elements (for example, brace with beam, or brace with purlin). The first class of joints is designated *tsugite* (splicing joints), and the second class *shiguchi* (connecting joints). Both types of joint are made to withstand tension and compression. The Japanese carpenter must take into account the total load-bearing capacity of the entire structure, thereby assuming responsibilities that in the West are commonly the domain of the architect.

The determining factor in the design of the rod mortise-and-tenon joints shown at right and on the facing page is the number of horizontal beams that have to be joined at the same height with a single post. Usually, two, three or four members are involved.

In the earliest forms of the joint, the horizontal members were mortised into the receiving post across their entire cross section. In later versions, the extended rod tenon of one beam is inserted through the vertical post into a mortise cut into the end of a second beam. The tenon is secured with a

wedge inserted from above. The addition of a shoulder greatly increases the load-bearing capacity of the joint.

When new beams are added between existing posts, the necessary joints are often made with loose rod tenons (see p. 46).

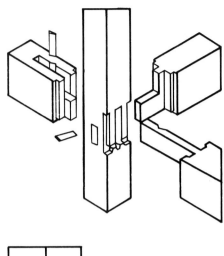

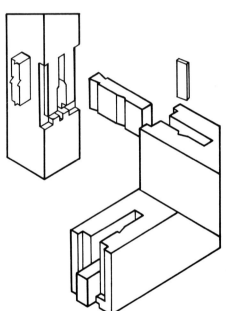

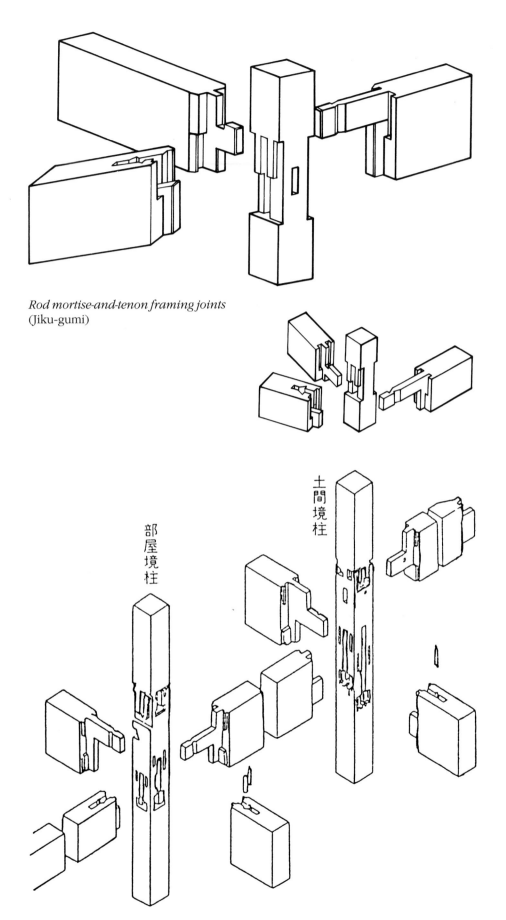

Rod mortise-and-tenon framing joints
(Jiku-gumi)

部屋境柱

土間境柱

Japanese drawings of framing joints

Tabled Splayed Joints

The **simple splayed scarf joint** is the starting point for a number of very solid, tension-resistant joints for splicing construction beams. When a table is added to the mating surfaces, the joint is better able to resist pullout. Because most **tabled splayed scarf joints** have identical mating parts, they are relatively easy to make. These joints are also called **hooked scarfs.**

The top drawing on the facing page shows a very stable hook joint that has tapered, dovetailed jaws to ensure against joint separation. The design prevents twisting and lateral shifting in one direction. When used on a load-bearing beam, this hook joint should always be supported from below to avoid splitting.

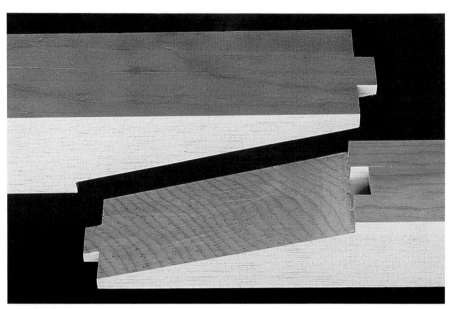

Susan Kahn

Splayed scarf joint with stub tenons (Daimochi-tsugi)

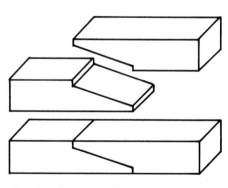

Simple splayed scarf joint

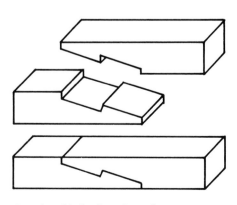

Simple tabled splayed scarf

Tabled splayed scarf with stub tenons, mortised to receive vertical post's tenon (Daimochi-tsugi-te)

The **tabled splayed scarf with stub tenons** is a very old Japanese purlin joint. The stub tenons prevent lateral shifting.

If a tabled scarf joint on a beam is positioned above or below a post, the post's tenon can be mortised through both lapping parts, thereby greatly increasing the joint's resistance to tension. If the joint is made on a sill resting on a wall, square-shaped pegs concealed within the joint ensure a stable joint.

The tabled scarf joint can also be made with rabbets, or lips, instead of stub tenons. The mating parts are slid together from the side. Reinforced with square pegs, this joint can withstand forces from all directions.

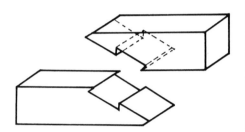

Hook scarf with tapered jaws

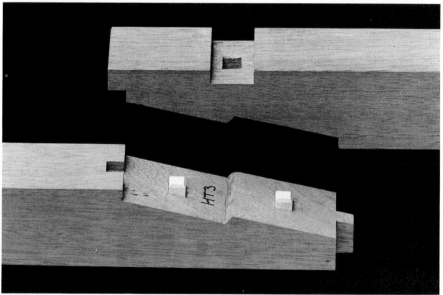

Tabled splayed scarf with stub tenons and blind pegs (Daimochi-tsugi)

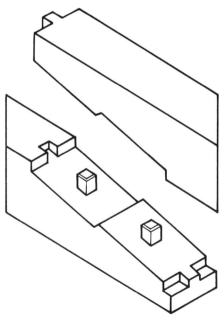

Tabled splayed scarf with stub tenons and blind pegs

Lipped tabled splayed scarf with pins (Okkake-dai-sen-tsugi)

The Gerber Joint

In 1880, Heinrich Gerber developed a special hooked scarf joint for joining purlins in civil engineering. The so-called **Gerber joint** is used to splice a purlin section into position from below. The joint, which is secured with bolts, has two advantages:

1. It can be used without a supporting post directly below the joint. The distance between the end of the spliced section and the nearest supporting post is ⅕ to ½ of the total bearing width. The purlin can be considered as load-bearing along its entire length, which simplifies arithmetic calculations.

2. Because the purlin section is installed from below, it protects the host purlin from splitting.

The Gerber joint can be further reinforced against tension by inserting hardwood keys, wedges or pegs.

The disadvantage of this joint is that it is difficult to position the inserted purlin section.

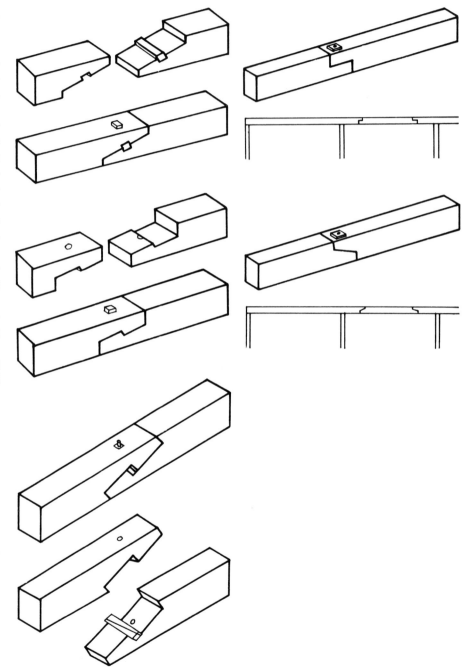

Variations of the Gerber joint

52

Tabled Lap Scarf Joints

Lap joints can also be tabled. In its basic form, the **lipped tabled lap scarf** has mating surfaces that are aligned vertically (compared with the tabled splayed joint, in which the alignment is horizontal). This orientation decreases stress on the rabbeted lips. The shoulders of the table are cut at a slight taper to prevent vertical shifting.

The **pegged tabled lap scarf** is sometimes known as the "arch clasp." Pegging the joint provides better resistance to vertical shifting than tapering the shoulders of the table. This joint is used for joining arched cornice boards and for joining rafters, and it is also used in interior work.

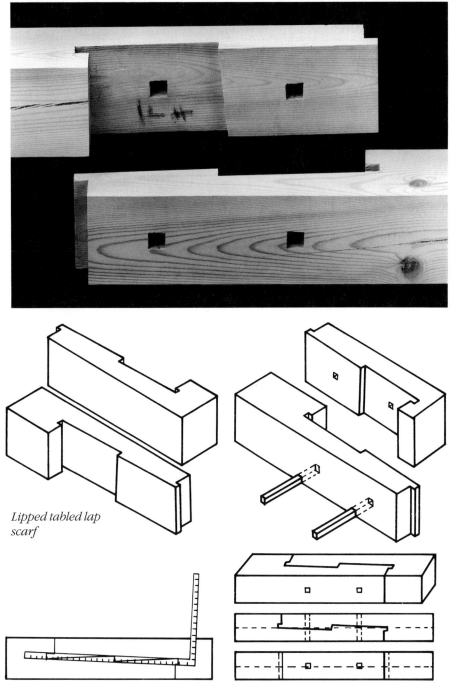

Lipped tabled lap scarf

Layout using the 15-mm (⅝-in.) wide Japanese square

Lipped tabled lap scarf reinforced with pegs (Atsukake-daisen-tsugi)

The **wedged arch clasp** can be used as a splicing joint for timbers joined at low angles (less than 60° from the axis). One application of this joint is for splicing barge boards at the ridge.

In addition to the tabled lap joints that are made by sliding the mating parts together from the side, there are variations that are fit together from above. The simplest design, which is used for supported sills and top plates, is the **cogged lap joint with straight shoulders.** The cogs, which are small tables or thick tongues, should be at least 10 cm to 12 cm (4 in. to 4¾ in.) long to ensure sufficient stability along the shear surface.

In cases where beams are too short to permit any kind of overlapping joint, a **bridled cog joint** may be the solution. This joint is reliable only on solidly supported sills, which must be load-bearing to prevent twist.

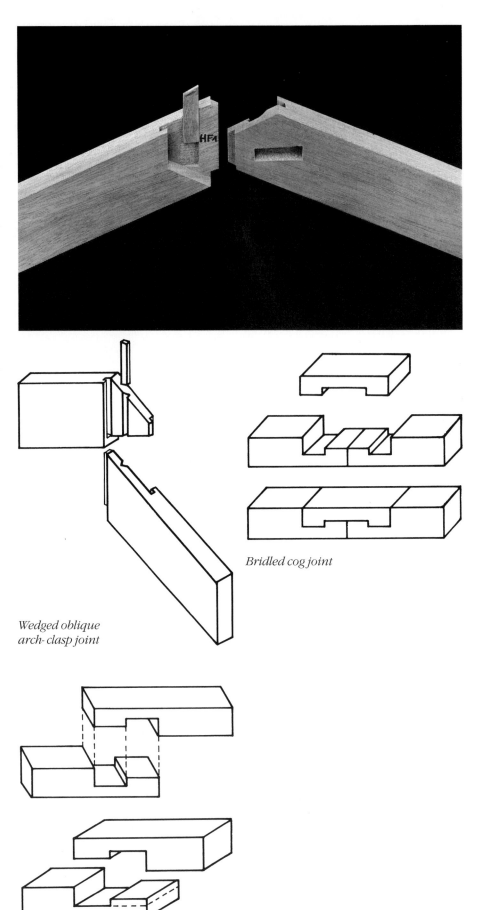

Bridled cog joint

Wedged oblique arch-clasp joint

Cogged lap joint with straight shoulders

Cogged joints for timber framing

The joints shown here, which are based on the principle of the cogged lap, are some of the oldest Japanese joints used in timber framing. As mentioned earlier, two or more beams are often mortised through load-bearing vertical posts to create a strong, tension-resistant joint. These joints, which are relatively easy to construct, serve to tie the whole building together. They are also advantageous from an aesthetic viewpoint, because the joints are concealed in the post and several beams can be joined at the same level.

Japanese interlocking cogged joints are wedged to provide the compression necessary for their stability. As with rod mortise-and-tenon framing joints (see pp. 48-49), cutting the mortises in the posts does not significantly weaken the uprights. The tenons are so tightly wedged in their mortises that the posts are immovable.

Splaying the jaws of the cogged lap makes it possible to slide two beams into each other for a perfect fit within the post (as shown in the drawing at far right). However, the beams can be joined in only one direction. Where timbers must be joined from two directions at the same height, the shoulders of the mating posts are also splayed (see the drawing at near right).

With a gooseneck-tenon joint, a wooden pin is used instead of a wedge to secure the mating beams to the post.

If a sill that will support floor-framing beams is joined to a vertical post, a haunched tenon on the end of the sill is housed in the post's mortise and reinforced with wooden keys (see the bottom drawing on p. 56).

Interlocking splayed cogged joints (Yonnai-gana *and* Ninai-gana, *or* Shiho-kama *and* Nimai-kama)

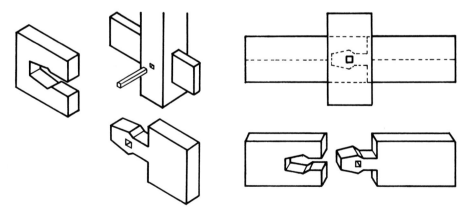

Pinned gooseneck joints (Kanasen-uchi, *or* Komisen-uchi)

Wedged cogged lap joint

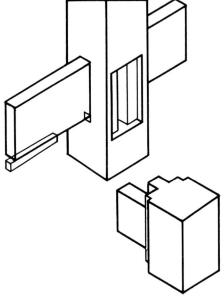

Keyed housed sill with haunched tenon
(Nuki-shiho-zashi)

Tabled Joints with Wedges

All of the tabled and cogged splicing joints discussed so far can be made to accept wedges. Wedging can ensure the permanent stability of joints, but there are a number of things to bear in mind:

1. Because wood has a longitudinal tubular cell structure, it can withstand a great compression load along its length without its fibers being crushed. Resistance to compression perpendicular to the grain, however, is much less great. Because wedges enter the joint at right angles to the grain of the mating parts, their fibers are exposed to lateral compression. If a joint is subject to tension, the wedges may no longer be able to resist compression and the fibers may break.

2. If the wedges shrink, the joint will lose its precision fit. For this reason, wedges should be made from extremely dry wood, which has the additional advantage of being more resistant to compression than green wood. Atmospheric humidity causes dry wedges to swell, which compensates somewhat for joint shrinkage.

3. Bridled cogged joints should be used only if they are solidly supported below, because they offer no resistance to deflection.

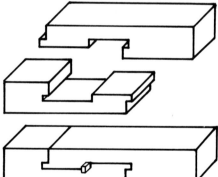

Wedged lipped tabled lap joint (Kane-gata-ai-gaki-tsugi)

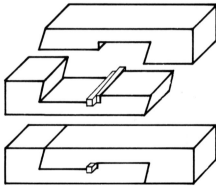

Wedged tabled lap joint with undercut shoulders

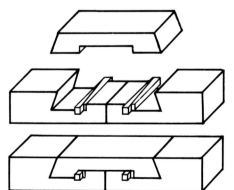

Bridled cogged lap joint with undercut shoulders and wedged keys

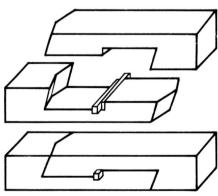

Self-centering tabled lap joint with wedged keys

Wedged locking joints

The **French lock joint,** a further refinement of the tabled lap joint, has a stub tenon added to the rabbet, which creates a T-shaped mortise and tenon. This joint must be wedged. The T-shaped tenon protects against buckling in heavily stressed posts and also prevents lateral shifting and twisting. As long as the joints are carefully made, the load-bearing capacity of beams spliced with locking joints is almost as great as it is for solid, continuous timbers. These joints are easily disassembled.

Visible joints can be partly concealed by making the stub tenons toward the inside (see the drawing below right).

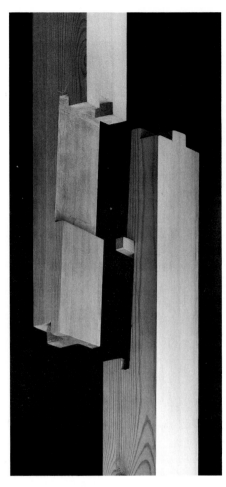

Half-blind tabled joints

Japanese carpenters and cabinetmakers devised other variants of tabled splicing joints that reveal only a simple straight or oblique joint line on exposed sides.

Half-blind tabled lap scarfs are typically used on facing boards, such as barge boards, eaves and cornices, but they can also be used on load-bearing beams. These joints are particularly effective for joining the arched boards of roof cornices, because they can withstand the tension caused by bending.

The **half-blind tabled lap scarf** is such a stable joint that it can be used over openings without support. It can also be used to lengthen projecting beams.

The **half-blind keyed tabled scarf with lips and stub tenons** is used for replacing sections of beams that are exposed to the weather.

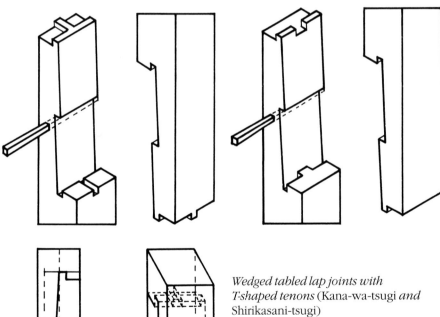

Wedged tabled lap joints with T-shaped tenons (Kana-wa-tsugi *and* Shirikasani-tsugi)

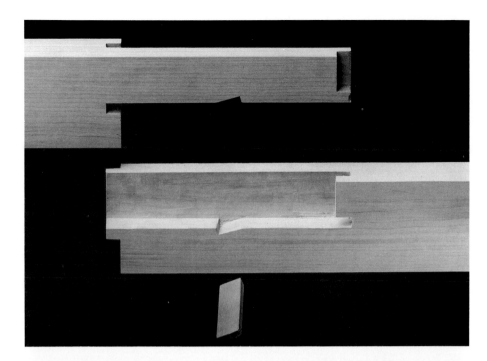

Half-blind keyed lap scarf
with lips and stub tenons
(Ni-men-kana-wa-shachi-sen-tsugi-te
or Hakodai-mochi-tsugi)

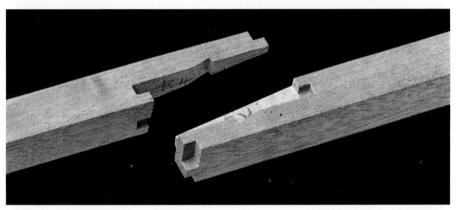

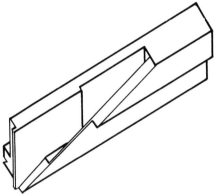

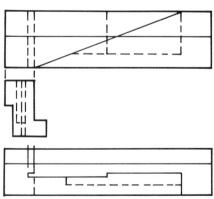

Half-blind tabled splayed scarf
with lips and stub tenons
(Ni-men-kana-wa-dai-sen-tsugi-te)

When splicing thick construction timbers that are square in cross section, the Japanese use a **half-blind tabled scarf with locking keys.**

The tabled or cogged effect can be achieved by inserting a wedge or key obliquely across the grain. This creates a very stable joint, which can even be used to splice corner posts.

Joints cut diagonally, as exemplified by the **blind diagonal lipped lap joint** used on freestanding posts, are particularly noteworthy. Cutting the joint on the diagonal creates a larger mating-surface area. With the help of modern machinery, miters and keyways are easy to cut accurately. The longitudinal joint lines blend in with the grain along the corners of the post. All that is visible on the four faces of the beam is a single cut perpendicular to the grain. The key is inserted diagonally through opposite corners.

Half-blind tabled scarf with lips and locking keys (Ni-ho-shachi-sen *or* Hakosen-tsugi)

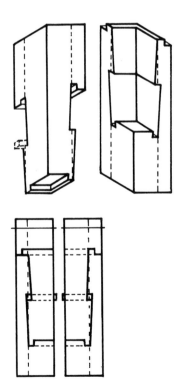

60

Half-blind lap joint with lips and diagonal keys (Ni-ho-dai-sen-tsugi-te *or* Hako shachi-tsugi)

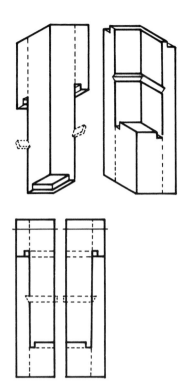

Blind diagonal lipped lap joint with single key (Hako-tsugite-shachi-sen)

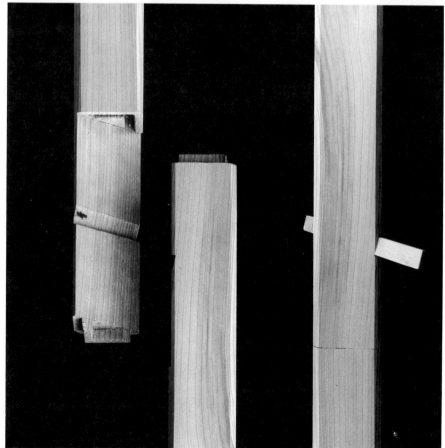

Offset knee braces joined with sloped mortise and tenons

2 Oblique Joints

An oblique joint is used to join two pieces of wood that meet at an angle less than 90°.

Oblique joinery is of secondary importance in Japanese wood construction, and the joints are relatively unrefined. In the West, by contrast, oblique joints are used extensively in the construction of roofs, houses and bridges, and in civil engineering. Oblique joints are indispensable in triangulated wood structures, where they are used, for example, on knee braces, struts and supporting braces for rafters, collar ties and straining beams.

Oblique joinery is also used in cabinetmaking to increase structural rigidity. An example is the joint made between a brace and a batten on a door.

The choice of joint is determined by the amount of stress it must withstand. Wall braces that carry light loads are usually joined to posts and beams with a notched mortise and tenon, which is nailed or pegged to counter tension and compression. In modern construction, nailing and pegging are often omitted, which significantly reduces the effectiveness of the joint.

Braces used in the roof framework are subject to greater stress and are secured with different forms of the basic notched joint. Calculating the angle of the brace, the depth of the notch and the distance between the front shoulder of the notch and the end of the supporting beam requires the use of engineering tables.

Rafters require numerous oblique joints, such as the bird's-mouth joint between rafters and purlins and the various notched joints used to connect jack rafters, hip rafters, the top plate and the ridge.

Oblique notched joints are occasionally used for right-angle joinery, as in the case of the wall-framing joints shown on p. 75. Parallel beams can also be joined with notched joints to form a beam of double the cross section (see pp. 72-74).

Notched Joints

A notched joint is used to form a compression-resistant connection between timbers that meet at an oblique angle. The joint's forward shoulder bears most of the load. Because wood is highly resistant to compression parallel to the grain, this joint can withstand relatively large loads.

The mating surfaces of the notch must be cut with utmost precision to avoid excessive stress on isolated parts of the joint that could cause splitting along the grain.

The **notched heel joint** is the basic form of oblique joinery. The angle of the front shoulder is critical and is determined according to technical and statistical criteria.

Load-bearing capacity is enhanced when the mating surfaces of the brace and the receiving timber are cut at the same angle. In this way, the angle of the front shoulder bisects the angle between the brace and beam (see the bottom drawing at right).

Technically, however, it is best if the front and rear shoulders of the notch form a right angle (as shown in the second drawing from the top at right). The advantage is that the right-angle notch can be cut in the beam precisely with the bird's-mouth cut positioned at an oblique angle. If the angle between the front and rear shoulders does not equal 90°, final fitting is more difficult. Although cutting the notch at a right angle results in an unequal distribution of load on the end of the brace and the beam, the disadvantage is not significant.

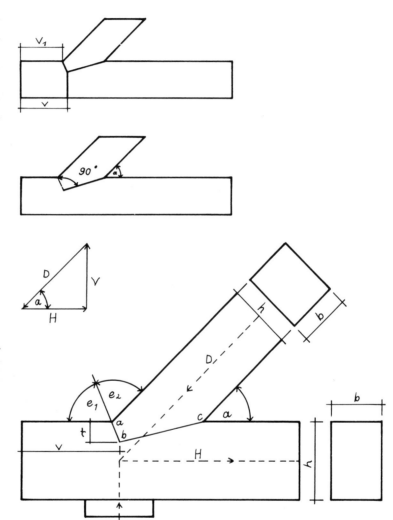

Notched heel joint (Kashigi-oire)
D = *compression on brace*
H = *horizontal tension on beam ($H = D \cos a$)*
V = *vertical load on bearing point ($V = D \sin a$)*
α = *brace or joint angle*
t = *notch depth*
v = *active shear surface length*
ab = *length of front shoulder*
bc = *length of rear shoulder*

Shear stress is greatest at the deepest point of the front shoulder. The calculation must take into account the distance from the front shoulder to the member's end (v).

Notch depth

To avoid weakening the receiving beam, the notch should not be cut too deeply. For oblique joints less than 50°, the notch should be no more than one-quarter the thickness of the beam. For joints between 50° and 60°, the notch depth should be between one-quarter and one-sixth the beam thickness; and for joints greater than 60°, no more than one-sixth the thickness.

If a notch is cut on two sides of a timber, each notch should have a maximum depth of one-sixth the thickness of the timber, regardless of the angle of the joint.

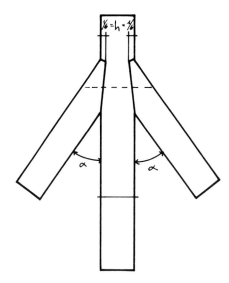

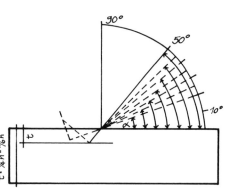

Uneven shear stress results when the active shear surface is too long.

Active shear surface

When a brace is joined to a timber, the notch must be set back a certain distance from the end of the beam so that the wood between the front shoulder and the beam end does not split under the force of compression. The wood in front of the notch is known as the "active shear surface."

The load that a notched joint can carry depends to a large extent on the length of the active shear surface. If this part of the beam is too short, it will split under the compressive force of the brace. The distance between the notch and the beam end should be at least 20 cm (8 in.), because the checks and cracks that commonly occur in the end grain of the beam further reduce resistance to shear stress. However, a shear surface that is too long causes an uneven distribution of shear stress on the beam.

A rough rule of thumb to calculate the ideal shear-surface length is that the distance from the deepest point of the notch to the end of the beam should be eight times the depth of the notch.

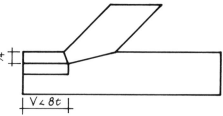

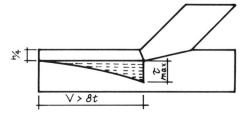

The shaded section shows the distribution of shear stress.

Notched mortise and tenons

Whereas civil engineers normally use wooden pins or bolts to secure notched heel joints against shifting and twisting, carpenters use a tenon to prevent joint failure. For mortise-and-tenon joints to seat properly, it is imperative that the mortise be 1 mm (⅟₁₆ in.) deeper than the tenon. This ensures that the compression load is transferred through the mating shoulders of the joint.

When calculating the angle of the brace, it is important to bear in mind that the load-bearing capacity of the joint is reduced by cutting the mortise in the beam. To reinforce the joint, the tenon on the end of the brace should be pegged. The ends of the tenon should be cut back at the same angle as the mating surfaces of the notch.

In Japan, the preferred form of the joint is the **notched mortise and tenon** (see the top drawing at right). The shoulder of the tenon is oriented so that it bisects the angle between the brace and the beam. It is cut back so that it crosses the centerline at the deepest point of the notch. In this way, the forces of the brace are transferred centrally along the beam.

Slot mortise and tenons

A **slot mortise and tenon** can be used instead of a notched joint. The advantage of this joint is that it can withstand lateral stress. Although the mortised beam is not weakened as much as in the simple notched joint, the load-bearing capacity of the brace's slot tenon is about three times less. The slot mortise and tenon should also be pinned.

Slot mortise and tenons are often used on knee braces between posts and the top plate, where the load is not too great. A disadvantage of this joint, however, is that it can open when the wood shrinks or twists.

To add bracing to an existing structure, the outside corner of the tenon must be cut back at a steep angle, as shown in the drawings at right of the **beveled slot mortise and tenon.**

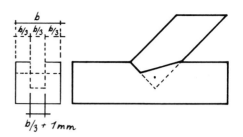

Notched mortise and tenon

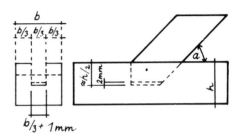

Slot mortise and tenon (Nagare-hozo)

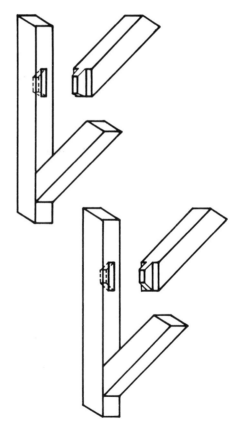

Beveled slot mortise and tenon

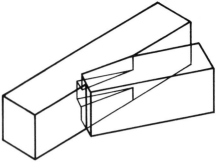

Notched mortise and tenon
(Kashigi-oire)

Susan Kahn

Susan Kahn

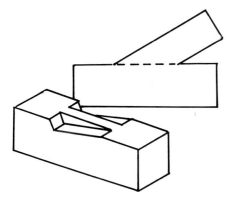

The slotted notched heel joint, which prevents lateral slippage of roof braces, can support greater loads than the slot mortise and tenon.

Offset knee braces joined with sloped mortise and tenons (Ari-otoshi)

Shouldered heel joints

In cases where the active shear surface is not long enough to allow use of a simple notched heel joint, the load-bearing point of the notch can be moved farther from the timber's end by using a **shouldered heel joint.** The forward shoulder (shaded in the drawings below and at top right) is often left on the brace for aesthetic reasons. In this case, however, a slight opening should be left between the shoulder and the beam, so that load on the shoulder does not split the brace. In the shouldered heel joint, the active axis coincides with the longitudinal axis of the brace, thereby eliminating the possibility of brace deflection caused by an eccentric load.

If the brace enters the supporting beam at a low angle, the notch for the simple heel joint can become critically deep. This problem can be overcome by using a **slope-shouldered heel joint.**

With the **straight-shouldered heel joint,** the notch can be set back even farther from the beam's end. Although this increases the length of the active shear surface, the brace is loaded eccentrically.

The **notched butt joint** is used on short or small-dimension braces.

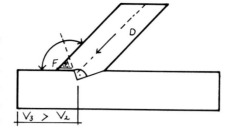

Slope-shouldered heel joint

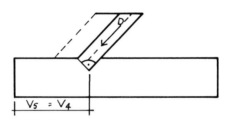

Straight-shouldered heel joint

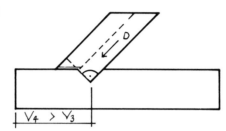

Notched butt joint

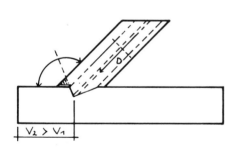

Shouldered heel joint

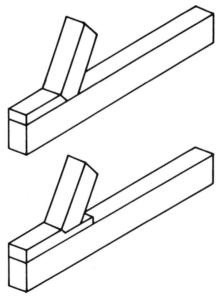

Sistered heel joints

Double-notched joints

If the notched joints discussed so far do not meet calculated stress requirements for withstanding compression or shear stress, it may be desirable to use a **double-notched joint.**

Cutting the double notch increases the surface area subjected to shear stress. Distortion caused by shrinkage is less significant than with the simple notched heel joint, which can open along the rear-shoulder surface as the wood shrinks, transferring compression load to the front shoulder. The resulting eccentric load is countered by deflection of the brace. There is no deflection with double-notched joints and shouldered heel joints, because they maintain their strength better than single heel joints as the wood shrinks.

The commonest form of the double-notch joint in use today is the **double-notched toe and heel joint.** There are many variations on this joint.

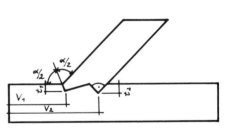

Double-notched toe and heel joint

There are a number of factors to consider when making double-notched joints:

1. Both the shoulder and the heel must seat firmly on their mating parts. This requires very precise fitting. If the timbers twist before they are assembled, they must be replaced.

Lead shims can be used to compensate for an inexact fit, but then the joint is not a notched joint in the true sense.

2. The shoulder notch should be cut 20% shallower than the heel notch. In this way, the two notches in the cross beam expose different grain surfaces to shear stress.

3. If the joint is secured with bolts, it is important to make sure that the washers are not located close to an edge and are properly countersunk. The bolts should be inserted at right angles to the line bisecting the angle of the brace and supporting beam.

Triple-notched joint

Triple-notched joints have exceptional load-bearing capacity, as long as they are used on timbers that are suitably large in cross section. As with the double-notched joints, precise fitting is essential to ensure that all joint surfaces mate exactly. These joints should be protected against lateral shifting with fishplates or bolts.

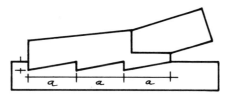

Triple-notched joint

Multiple-notched joints for toothed and splined girders

Wide spans and heavy loads sometimes require the use of girders with a larger cross section than can be found in a single tree. Even if large-dimension timbers are available, it is not advisable to use them because they are often deformed and cracked as a result of shrinkage. Instead, girders subject to heavy loads should be made of separate timbers joined parallel to the grain.

Today, large-dimension girders are usually made by gluing boards together under pressure. Producing these glue-lam beams is not very economical because the process is highly energy-intensive. The tree trunk must be sawn into boards, which must then be dried in kilns before being glued back together in huge presses. The beam must then be resawn to its final dimensions. The story does not end there. Only a few companies are able to produce laminated beams, which means that the raw materials must be transported to the manufacturer and the finished product subsequently delivered to the contractor.

Clearly, the use of toothed or splined girders assembled on the spot offers advantages, both in terms of cost and energy conservation.

The technique of joining girders with multiple-notched joints has been known in Europe for several hundred years. Examples are found in the stave churches of Scandinavia dating from the early Middle Ages, where the column shafts are enclosed by beams made of two timbers set next to each other and joined with splines. Toothed and splined beams were also used on wide-span wooden bridges built in Switzerland over 200 years ago. The fact that these bridges still carry today's heavy traffic is testimony to the strength of the multiple-notched joint.

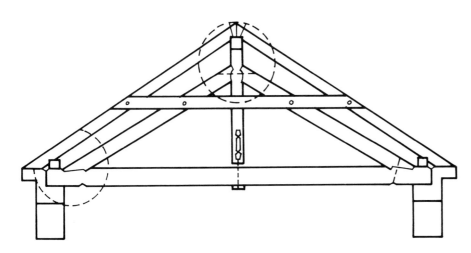

Suspension truss with double-notched joints

Toothed beams

The effectiveness of doubled beams is easy to explain. A beam with cross-sectional dimensions of 12 cm by 24 cm (4¾ in. by 9½ in.) can carry three times the load standing on edge as it can lying flat. Two beams placed on top of each other but not joined can support no more load than if they were placed side by side. However, when the two beams are solidly joined, their load-bearing capacity is more than tripled.

A solid joint can be made by cutting multiple notches along the mating surfaces of the two beams. The same technical rules apply for each individual notch of a toothed beam as for a simple notched heel joint.

To make a toothed girder, attention should be paid to the following factors:

1. The teeth on the lower beam should always be oriented with the end-grain surface pointing toward the center of the beam. The teeth on the upper beam point in the opposite direction.

2. The upper beam absorbs all the compression force. As a result, it can be made in several sections, which makes assembly easier.

3. Both beams should be bowed together when assembled. When the tension is released, the teeth are forced against each other firmly to ensure a tight seating.

4. The load-carrying capacity of toothed beams can be increased by bending the beams upward. Stressing the construction helps it to retain its raised-arch form. In this way, the forces from above are changed to forces of compression within the toothed beam acting on the notches parallel to the grain. Wood can withstand considerably more compression parallel to the grain than it can perpendicular to the grain. This inherent characteristic of wood can be used to great advantage in the construction of toothed beams. The increased resistance of toothed beams can be stress-tested with modern machinery (see the top photo on the facing page).

5. Compression stress between the two joined beams increases toward the ends of the beams. Accordingly, tooth spacing will be shorter over the bearing points than in the middle of the beam. This makes it possible to resolve a static problem that exists for conventional beams: Because bending stress on the beams is greatest midway between the two supports, the cross section of the entire beam must be concentrated on the load at this point. It thereby follows that each conventional beam is dimensionally larger toward the bearing points. With toothed beams, on the other hand, prestressing and unequal tooth spacing help to overcome this dimensional problem.

6. The upper and lower members of toothed beams must be secured with bolts and large washers or metal plates to prevent them from separating under load.

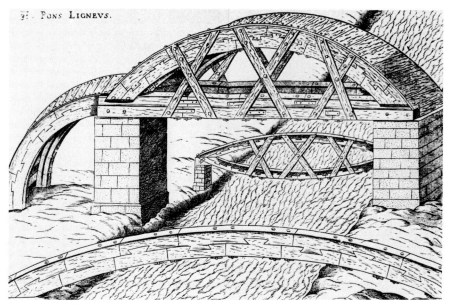

A Roman bridge

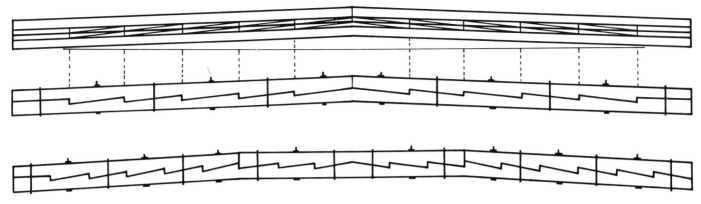

Toothed beams

Toothed beams being tested under stress

Contrary to intuition, notched teeth do not split under stress, whereas two solid beams placed together without notching would break in the middle in the same way as a single beam. (Photo by Firma Hotzenholz, Herrischried.)

Splined beams

Spline joinery is used to counteract forces of compression and shear stress. A splined beam is formed by joining two beams parallel to the grain by means of oak splines, ring connectors or shear plates. These fasteners prevent the two members from shifting against each other. Compression forms between the end grain of the cutouts on the beam and the splines. As a result, the splines and the active shear surfaces are subject to shear stress.

To prevent the splines and beams from moving perpendicular to the direction of force and the splines from tilting, the beams must be secured with bolts, cover plates or metal straps. Heavy-duty washers should be used with bolts to keep the bolts from pulling through wood. The resulting splined joint is not completely resistant to shear stress, and splined beams are consequently weaker than beams made from a single tree trunk.

Lacking data for precise measurement, the load-bearing capacity of a two-layered splined beam can be estimated as about 85% that of a solid beam of the same dimension; a three-layered beam has only 60% of the load-bearing capacity. Deflection in a two-layered splined beam is about 45% less than in its solid-wood counterpart. Thus, a two-layered splined beam is approximately 1.7 times stronger than two beams placed on top of each other but not joined, and its deflection is 2.5 times less.

The drawings at right show different methods of joining parallel beams with splines: with the splines inserted at an angle, across the grain and parallel to the grain.

Rectangular splines should be made of dry hardwood, and their length should be at least three times the depth of the notch in the beam. For the greatest absorption of compression, the grain direction of the splines and the beam should be parallel.

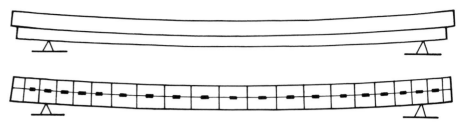

Unattached beams (top) and splined beams (above) under load. The splined beam is stronger and deflects less.

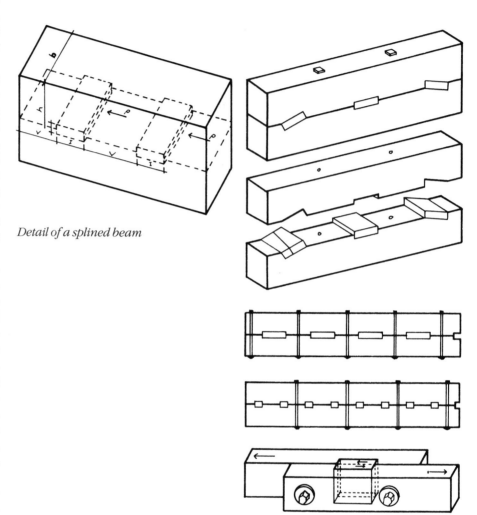

Detail of a splined beam

Middle section of a splined beam, with double and single splines

Right-angled notched joints

Horizontal members and posts in timber-frame walls are commonly connected with simple mortise-and-tenon joints. But when horizontal timbers must span wide openings and support heavy loads, the **beveled-shoulder notched mortise and tenon** is used. With this joint, the bearing surface of the tenoned member is increased, and the notch in the mortised post supports part of the load borne by the tenon. The notch also counters torsion in the horizontal member.

The tenon is normally 4 cm (1⅝ in.) wide and 4 cm to 5 cm long (1⅝ in. to 2 in.); the notch is then 1.5 cm to 2 cm (⅝ in. to ¾ in.) deep.

Right-angled notched joints are also used in roof trusses to connect collar ties and queen posts. The notched joint is oriented upward. In this application, the joint must be secured with nailed wood gussets.

Corner posts should be joined to the sill with **offset shouldered tenons** to prevent their separating as a result of lateral shear. This measure increases the active shear surface in front of the tenon. If the end of the sill is not allowed to project beyond the corner of the house, the active shear surface is too short to counter shear stress. A solution is to tie the sill into the corner post with a notched mortise-and-tenon joint, which will ensure a good seating and prevent lateral movement.

Because their end-grain surfaces are exposed, corner sill joints are particularly vulnerable to decay. Provided that thrust force is not a concern, it is advisable to extend the post as far down as possible and to tie the sill into it with a stub tenon and a shoulder angled upward. The tenons should be mortised deeply enough into the post so that they can be pinned crossways without splitting.

Susan Kahn

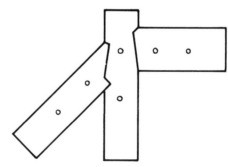

Beveled-shoulder notched mortise and tenon (Oire)

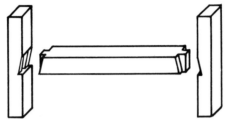

Roof truss with right-angled notched joint and oblique double-notched joint

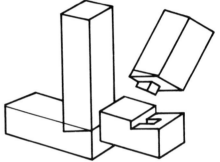

Notched corner-post joint with offset shouldered tenon

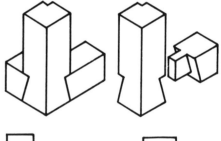

Notched corner-post joint with beveled-shoulder tenon

Bird's-Mouth Joints

A **bird's-mouth joint** is used to join a timber to the corner of an intersecting timber at an angle. The notch, or bird's mouth, in this joint is similar to that of the notched heel joint, but load transference is in the opposite direction.

Bird's-mouth joints, which are fastened with pegs or nails, are used primarily to connect rafters to plates and purlins. Because the bird's mouth weakens the rafter in cross section, it should be no deeper than one-quarter the total thickness of the rafter — generally, no more than 1.5 cm to 3 cm (⅝ in. to 1¼ in.) deep. The bird's mouth on the gable-end rafter should be cut only three-quarters of the way across the rafter's width. Stopping the notch short of the outside edge of the rafter protects the end grain of the purlin from exposure to the weather.

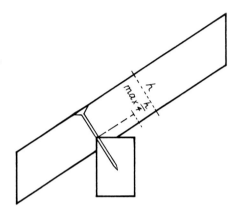

Bird's-mouth joint on a common rafter

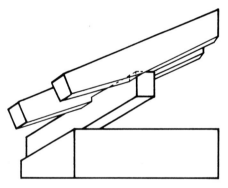

Bird's-mouth joint with a stopped mortise on a gable-end rafter

Oblique cuts and roof design

When roofing timbers intersect at oblique angles, as shown in the drawings on the facing page, calculating the angles and the lengths of the timbers is complicated. To determine the proportions of the angles within the joints, the lines of the corresponding roof sections must be projected onto the horizontal bottom surfaces. The laws of descriptive geometry play a major role in the calculation of trigonometric functions, angles and counter angles for oblique roofing timbers. For example, a bird's-mouth joint on a jack rafter is dependent on the pitch of the hip roof and the main roof, the length of the roof and the bearing height of the roof.

The geometrical proportions of the roof truss are reflected in the intersecting planes of the bird's mouth. Because it is impossible to mark out the true length of a beam projecting into space at an oblique angle, making joints on roofing timbers challenges the competence and imagination of even the most experienced carpenter.

Oblique notched joints are essential for the construction of hip roofs with jack rafters, which are found throughout the East and West. They are also important features of valley roofs and of any roof that has an irregular layout or uneven pitch.

On hip roofs, the jack rafters tie the wall plate or foot purlin to the hip rafter. They are fastened to the hip rafter from below, either with a simple oblique butt joint or with a bird's mouth or "claw" on the hip's corner. The method of attachment depends on the steepness of the angle. Jack rafters are joined to the valley rafter from below.

It is time-consuming to make the joints between the hip jack rafters and the purlin and between the valley jack rafters and the ridge. Some of the joints used are shown on the facing page and on p. 78.

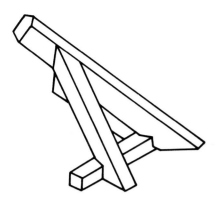

Hip jack rafter

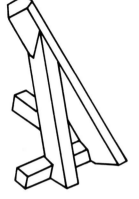

Notched hip jack rafter

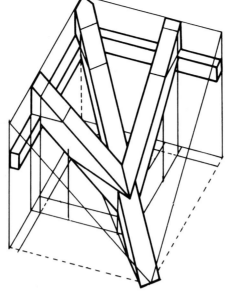

Valley rafter with notched jack rafters

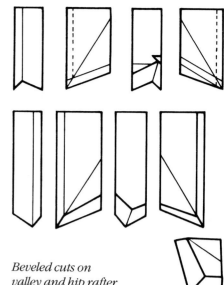

Beveled cuts on valley and hip rafter ends

Valley jack rafter

Notched valley jack rafter

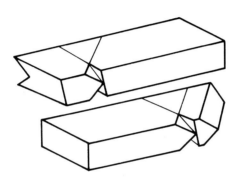

Valley and hip rafters prepared for assembly

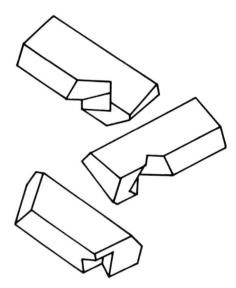

Hip-rafter bird's mouths

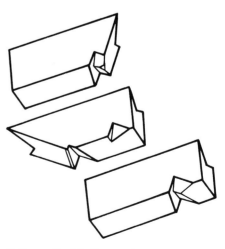

Valley-rafter bird's mouths

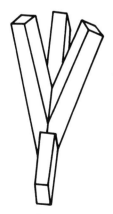

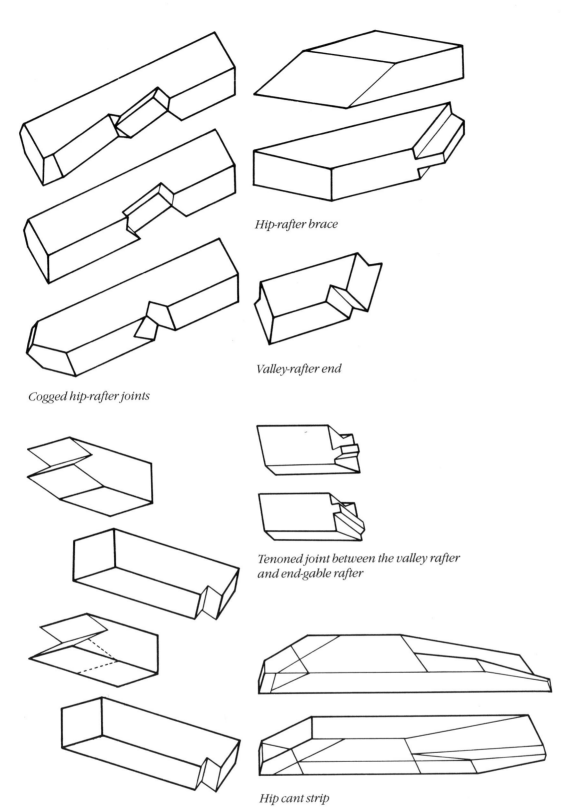

Hip-rafter brace

Cogged hip-rafter joints

Valley-rafter end

Tenoned joint between the valley rafter
and end-gable rafter

Claw joints, jack rafter to hip rafter
attachment

Hip cant strip

Angled Lap Joints

Although lap joints reduce the cross section of the mating members considerably, it is rare to find lap joints in old roof frames that have failed as a result of splitting, even if the timbers are relatively weak. It is also uncommon for lap joints to fail because their pegs work loose from the joint.

Angled lap joints are used to connect king posts and their supporting braces. For rigid bracing, where both compression and tension must be countered, **angled half-dovetail lap joints** are often used. Collar ties and rafters are also joined with half dovetails.

The **angled housed half-lapped dovetail** is an interesting Japanese joint that is unknown in the same form in the West. This joint, which can be used to add a brace to an existing structure, requires no nailing or other form of fastening. Furthermore, it does not significantly weaken the tenon on the brace, and it prevents the brace and post from pulling apart.

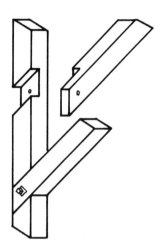

Angled lap joint

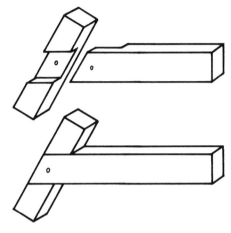

Angled lap joint on a collar tie

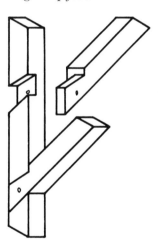

Angled half-dovetail lap joint

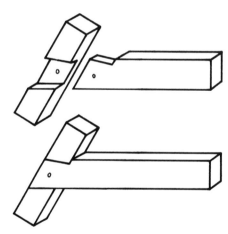

Angled half-dovetail lap joint on a collar tie

Angled housed half-lapped dovetail (Hiuchi-ari-otoshi)

*Haunched mortise and tenon with
mitered laps*

3 Corner and Cross Joints

Right-angled joints take the form of corner joints, T-shaped joints and cross joints. If mating beams or boards are joined through only part of their cross section (and consequently do not lie in the same plane), we talk of offset joints. In the following presentation, however, we focus on the evolution of the individual joint forms (such as the mortise and tenon, lap and cogged joint) and their various combinations in order to throw some light on the function of each joint.

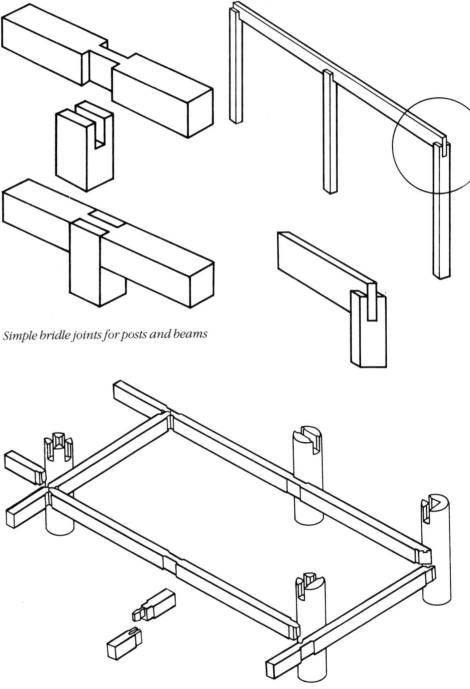

Simple bridle joints for posts and beams

Bridle joints used in Japanese temples
(Wanagi-komi)

Bridle Joints

The basic form of all right-angled joints is the fork, or groove, into which is inserted a perpendicular mating member. One of its simplest forms is the **bridle joint,** or slip joint, which has been known in the West since the time of the first northern European stave buildings and is still widely used in modern construction. A horizontal beam is housed in a fork cut in the end of a vertical support. The joint is secured with bolts or pegs.

Bridle joints used in furniture

Butt Joints

Mortise-and-Tenon Joints

In its simplest form, the right-angled **butt joint** can transfer forces of compression only. It can be modified to withstand lateral force by housing the post in the horizontal beam to a depth of 2 cm (¾ in.). Dowels can also be used to prevent shifting of the post, but this method provides little protection against twisting. This type of joint is used today in the wall frames of prefabricated houses. Reinforced with nails, the butt joint is the basic connection in frame carpentry.

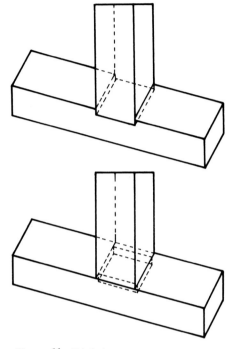

Housed butt joint

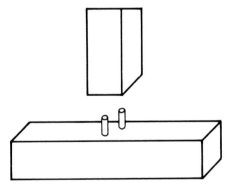

Doweled butt joint

The **mortise and tenon** is by far the the most commonly used right-angled joint. Its ease of construction and ability to withstand forces from several directions makes it an especially well-suited joint for connecting posts, beams, wall plates, sills and other members in timber-frame structures. Mortise-and-tenon joints are also used in the construction of cabinet frames, doors and windows, in stairbuilding and in countless other applications.

A tenoned post inserted vertically into a mortised beam secures the beam against lateral movement and prevents twisting. In modern timber framing, unpinned tenons are usually about 4 cm to 5 cm (1⅝ in. to 2 in.) long, and the mortise is cut about 0.5 cm (³⁄₁₆ in.) deeper then the length of the tenon. The clearance for the tenon end ensures that the tenon does not butt against the bottom of the mortise when the mating timber shrinks in cross section, which would transfer all the compression force to the tenon.

Most tenons used in timber framing are 4 cm (1⅝ in.) thick, in accordance with modern tool specifications. When deviating from this standard, the tenon's width should be one-third the width of its timber.

Mortises exposed to the weather, such as those cut in a groundsill, are prone to decay because they can trap moisture. To provide effective drainage, the mortises should be cut all the way through the beam or have drilled drainage holes. For additional protection, it's a good idea to use white oak for groundsills and other exposed beams.

If a tenon becomes loose as a result of shrinkage, the joint can be reinforced by inserting a hardwood wedge between the tenon and the side of the mortise. Joints subjected to tension can be secured with wooden fishplates or treenails. Pegged joints are used on wall partitions in light timber-frame construction. The rigidity of the wall can be reinforced by pegging the wall plates and both ends of the braces. To relieve lateral compression force on the corner posts, some of the intermediate wall posts can also be pegged. Pegged joints require tenons that are 2 cm to 3 cm (¾ in. to 1¾₁₆ in.) longer than usual to prevent the treenail from splitting the tenon.

The plain mortise and tenon, which is the most widely used form of the joint, transfers forces through the shoulders of the tenon. **Sloped mortise and tenons** are used to join corner posts to the sill and wall plate. Sloping the outside cheek of the tenon leaves more wood between the mortise and the end of the sill, which prevents the corner post from shifting outward under lateral compression. Tapering the tenon toward the end of the sill further strengthens the joint, though great care must be taken when making the angled cuts. An ill-fitting tenon may cause the sill end to split under the load of the post.

Door posts should be treated in the same way as corner posts, because an existing sill is often cut to allow for the door opening. It is important to make sure that the sloped cheek is cut on the correct side of the tenon, or the joint will lose its lateral stability.

Continuous sills and wall plates can be tied at the corner posts with **right-angled mortise and tenons.** These corner joints prevent the posts from twisting and shifting.

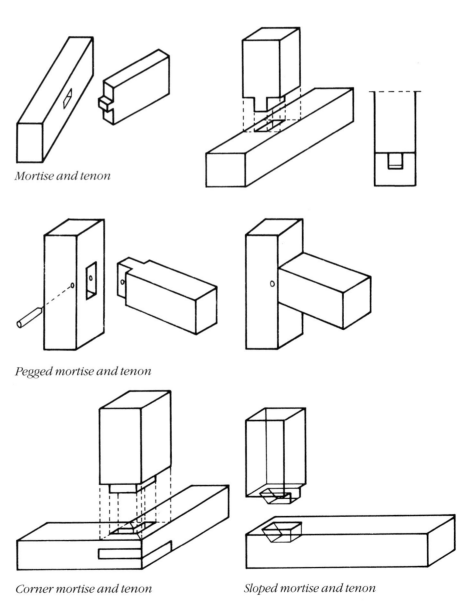

Mortise and tenon

Pegged mortise and tenon

Corner mortise and tenon

Sloped mortise and tenon

Large-dimension posts can be joined to narrower sills by combining a mortise and tenon and a lap joint, as shown in the drawing below.

Depending on the loads they must carry, joints between horizontal members such as joists, headers and lintels can be made with **simple mortise and tenons, straight housed mortise and tenons, sloped housed mortise and tenons** or **tusk tenons.** The tenoned members should be housed no deeper than 1.5 cm to 2 cm (⅝ in. to ¾ in.) to avoid weakening the receiving beams.

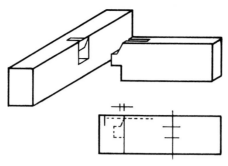

Sloped housed mortise and tenon (Kiba-hozo)

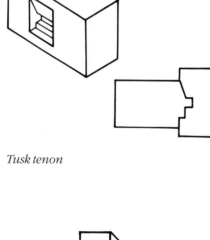

Tusk tenon

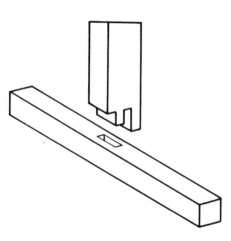

Mortise and tenon with a lap on one side

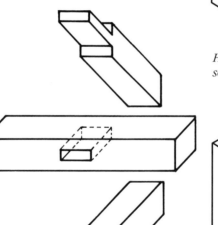

Through tenons for light framing and furniture making

Haunched mortise and tenons

The mortise-and-tenon joints shown below and on the facing page are commonly used in the West and in Japan, both in construction and in cabinet-making. The **haunched mortise and tenon** is used in preference to the sloped mortise and tenon (see p. 85) to add strength close to the end grain on corner joints. A similar joint known in the West is the **grooved through mortise and tenon.** Both joints ensure strong frames that are resistant to racking.

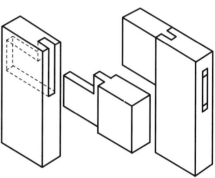

Haunched through mortise and tenon, sometimes wedged

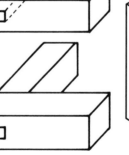

Through mortise and tenon with sloped haunch

Simple mortise and tenon with cramp iron

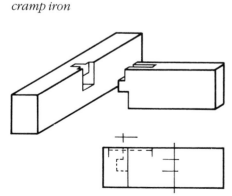

Straight housed mortise and tenon

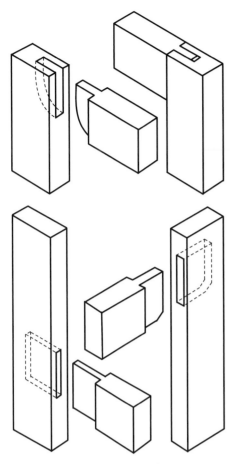

Bored, chopped and routed mortises

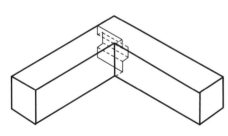

Lapped stub tenon (Mechigai-dome)

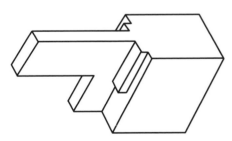

Cogged haunched mortise and tenon
(Eriwa-hozo)

Open slot mortise and tenon (Hira-hozo)

Offset mortise and tenon (Usu-hozo)

Haunched mortise and tenon (Kone-hozo)

Wedged mortise and tenons

Wedged blind mortise and tenon joints are made by loosely inserting wedges into kerf cuts in the end grain of the tenon, then driving the tenon into a slightly tapered mortise. When the wedges bottom out in the mortise they force the sides of the tenon against the tapered mating surfaces. Because the tenon is seated in a dovetail-shaped mortise, it is impossible to remove. This technique is sometimes called "fox-wedging."

Wedged through tenons, which are used on simple substructures hidden from sight, work in a similar way. Thin, hardwood wedges are driven into the end grain of the tenon, spreading it and wedging it securely in the tapered mortise. The wedges create an exceptionally stable joint and provide good resistance to tension.

Wedged blind mortise and tenons (Jigoku-kusabi)

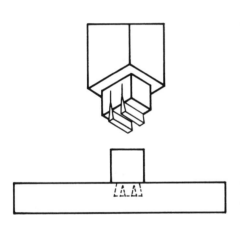

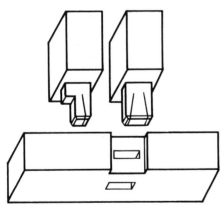

Wedged mortise and tenons (Kone-hozo *and* Koshi-tsuki)

Triple-wedged through tenon (Jigoku-hozo-sashi)

88

Draw-pin joints

In Japanese wood construction, the tenon almost always extends beyond the mortise in the receiving beam. This method of construction facilitates drainage of water from the joint and also makes it possible to lock the joint with a draw pin through the projecting tenon. In the West, this joint is used to make knockdown structures such as trestle tables and weaver's looms.

Depending on the length of the tenon, the pin can be inserted through its thickness (top photo at right) or through its width (bottom photo). The latter joint requires a longer tenon to prevent the pin from splitting the tenon. Through mortise and tenons pinned perpendicular to the tenon are often fitted with two pins to provide greater stability (see the top photo on p. 90). If the tenoned timber is not long enough to allow use of external draw pins, the tenon can be pinned through the mortised timber, as shown in the middle photo at right. Housing the joint increases its load-bearing capacity.

Draw-pin joints are suitable for stringers and sill joints, but also for furniture and frames. The wood used should be roughly square in section, and the thickness of the tenon must correspond to the load it will bear.

External draw-pin joint, pinned perpendicularly

Housed draw-pin joint (Komi-sen)

External draw-pin joint, pinned longitudinally (Tate-ippon-sen-hozo)

Multiple tenons

The **triple mortise and tenon** provides good protection against twisting and is often used between uprights and the frieze. This joint offers a greater glue surface area then the single mortise and tenon. When working with tenons that are small in cross section, joint openings caused by wood shrinkage are relatively unimportant, although they are difficult to avoid entirely even in wood that is air-dried.

The **quadruple mortise and tenon** provides an even larger surface area for gluing, but it is more difficult to make.

Through tenon with double draw pins (Yoko-ni-hon-sen-hozo)

Triple tenon with lateral mortise for oblique brace joint (Wanagi-hozo)

Triple mortise and tenon (Tate-san-mai-hozo)

Quadruple mortise and tenon (Tate-yon-mai-hozo)

Double tenons with coped shoulders

On interior finish work, coped joints and joinery with profiles and counter-profiles used to fit moldings together are good ways to improve both joint stability and appearance.

The **double mortise and tenon with coped shoulders** has a tenoned member whose profiled shoulders match the bevels on the edges of the mortised post. If the joint opens slightly, the opening is not visible from the outside.

The **housed double mortise and tenon** is a stronger version of the same joint. It is commonly used to connect the stiles, rails and mullions on window sash and similar frames.

A further refinement is to add mitered counter profiles to the housed double mortise and tenon, as shown in the bottom photo near right. The mitered cuts help to conceal any opening of the joint as a result of wood shrinkage.

Double mortise and tenons are used not only as T-joints but also as corner joints. The **blind mitered double mortise and tenon** shown in the drawing below is a particularly subtle corner joint used on built-in furniture, high-quality window frames and other furniture frames. With this joint, no end grain is visible.

Double mortise and tenon (Ni-mai-hozo) *and double mortise and tenon with coped shoulders* (Koshi-oshi-ni-mai-hozo)

Housed double mortise and tenon (Uma-nori-ni-mai-hozo) *and double housed double mortise and tenon* (Kuchi-uma-ni-mai-hozo)

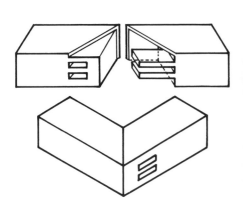

Blind mitered double mortise and tenon (Hako-dome)

Housed double mortise and tenon with mitered counter profiles

Mitered double mortise and tenon (Furi-dome/San-mai-hozo)

Open mortise-and-tenon joints

Open mortise-and-tenon joints, also known as **slot** or **slip mortise and tenons** or **tongue-and-fork joints,** are used in roof construction to join purlins at the corners. They are not good joints to use on sills, because the end grain is exposed to the weather.

Cabinetmakers use open mortise-and-tenon joints on frames when durability and rigidity are more important than appearance. They are not suitable for use on quality furniture because of the problems caused by unequal wood shrinkage across and along the grain. As the mortised member shrinks across its width, the end of the tenon will project beyond the mortise and the shoulders may open.

On window or door frames, the tenons should always be made on the horizontal rails and the mortises on the vertical stiles. If a door frame is rabbeted, the depth of the rabbet must be taken off the tenon on one side, as shown in the bottom drawing below.

Tapered open mortise-and-tenon joints

Cutting a taper on at least one side of the open mortise and tenon leaves a better looking joint, and will prevent any unsightly opening at the shoulder.

In frame-and-panel furniture, the panels are housed in grooves or rabbets in the frames, which are usually joined with open mortise-and-tenon joints. These joints may also be made with blind mortise-and-tenon joints, cut with a haunch to fill the groove.

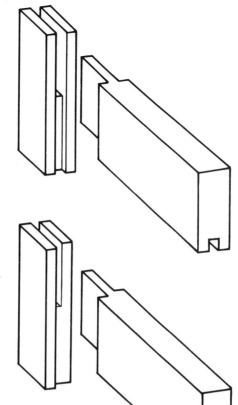

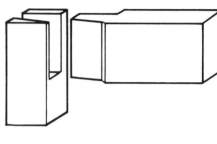

Tapered open mortise and tenon

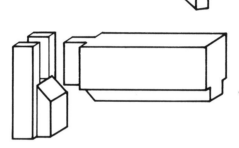

Frame-and-panel corner joints

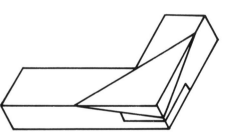

Corner joint concealed with an insert (for use on veneered frames)

Open mortise and tenon
(Kanegata-sanmai-hozo)

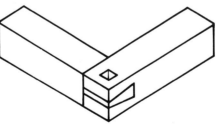

Through dovetail tenon with pin
(Ari-kata-sanmai-hozo-konisen-uchi)

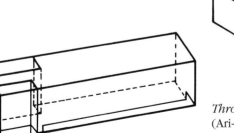

Open mortise and tenon for rabbeted door frame

92

Mortise-and-tenon joints for rafter roofs

The two main types of roofs are rafter roofs and purlin roofs.

Rafter roofs are traditionally found on stave or truss buildings. All load is transferred directly from the rafters to the longitudinal walls. Collar ties, cross bracing or struts connected to the rafters counter tension stress on the roof truss.

In this type of construction, rafters are typically joined at the peak using an open mortise and tenon. The joint is sometimes mitered on one side, as shown in the bottom drawing at right.

Half-lap joints for purlin roofs

During the Middle Ages, purlin roofs were considered inferior to rafter roofs in Europe. Today, however, they are widely used both in the West and in the East. In this type of construction, the load of the rafters is transferred through notched joints to a supporting framework of purlins. Because the rafters rest on a ridge pole, or ridge purlin, at the peak, a mortise-and-tenon joint is unnecessary; a simple half lap will do.

Wedged mitered open mortise-and-tenon joint with stub tenons for barge-board peak

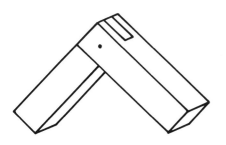

Open mortise and tenon for rafter peak

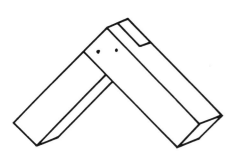

Half-lap joint for rafter peak on purlin roofs

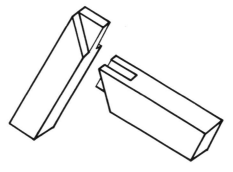

Open mortise and tenon, mitered on one side

Mitered mortise-
and-tenon joints

A mitered joint is one whose joint line bisects the angle at the corner of the two mating members. Mitered mortise-and-tenon joints have a number of advantages:

1. At sill corners, the mitered joint is concealed beneath the upright post, which provides good protection from the weather.

2. Because wood movement in the mitered mating members is relatively uniform, the joint should not open along the joint line.

3. A mitered joint makes a softer transition between two timbers meeting at a right angle. The grain of each piece flows into the other, instead of abruptly changing direction as in a simple butt joint. In addition, the end grain is completely concealed.

The miters should be slightly undercut, so that the outer tips do not move apart as the wood shrinks.

Mitered mortise and tenon (Furi-dome)

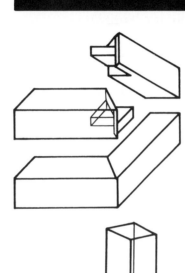
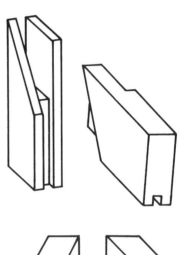
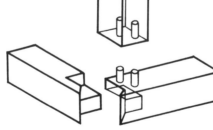
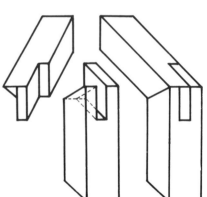

Blind mitered joints

Open mortise and tenon, mitered on one side

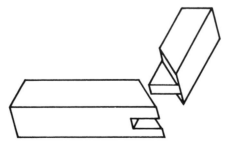
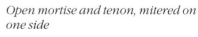

Half-blind mitered mortise and tenon (Tomekata-sanmai-hozo)

Blind mitered joints can be pinned through their tenons. These corner joints are used on window frames, shutters and door frames, in frame-and-panel construction and also on sill corners.

Half-blind mitered mortise-and-tenon joints, either grooved or rabbeted, make it possible to conceal corner joints on one side. Common applications are for coping, window and door frames and balcony railings.

The **half-blind mitered double mortise and tenon** is a Japanese refinement of the above joint. It is a very stable joint suitable for use on exposed frames and also for corner sill joints in log construction.

The **half-blind mitered haunched mortise and tenon** is a further variation of the concealed corner joint. Although it is not as stable as some of the other mitered mortise-and-tenon joints, it is aesthetically pleasing and provides excellent end-grain protection. The through tenon can be wedged from the outside, but care must be taken to avoid splitting the end of the mortised member.

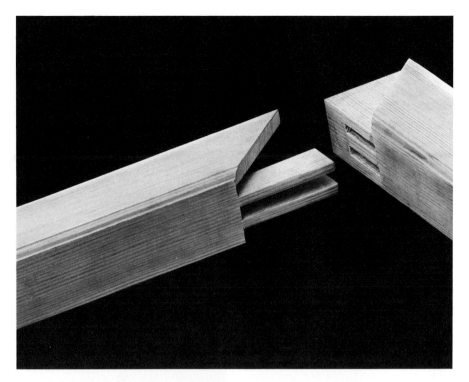

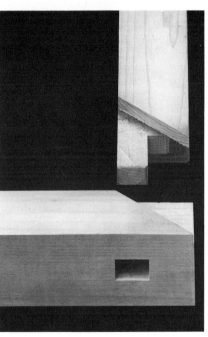

Half-blind mitered haunched double and simple mortise and tenons (O-dome)

Through tenons are not suitable for furniture that will be coated with finishes such as varnish. Uneven wood movement between the tenon end and its mortise will eventually crack the finish at the joint.

Haunched mortise and tenon with stop-mitered lap and stub tenons

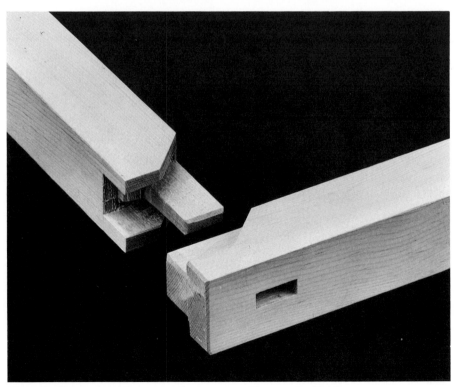

Haunched mortise and tenon with stop-mitered laps on both sides

Housed mortise-
and-tenon joints

Housed mortise-and-tenon joints, which are known in various forms in both the East and the West, are designed to prevent movement in one direction. Cabinetmakers use them as glue joints to assemble boards of narrow thickness. When reinforced with threaded rods or bolts, they are also useful construction joints.

Some Japanese forms of these joints have mitered laps, and stub tenons are sometimes added to prevent twisting.

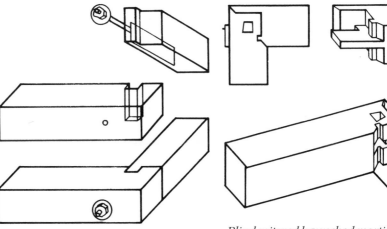

Housed tenon with tensioning bolt (Eriwa)

Blind mitered haunched mortise and tenon with stub tenons (Sumidome-hozo-sashi)

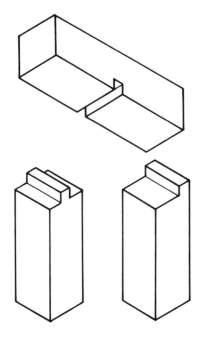

Housed mortise and tenons (Michi-giri)

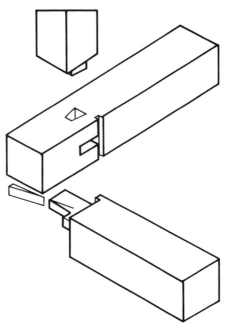

Wedged haunched mortise and tenon with stub tenon

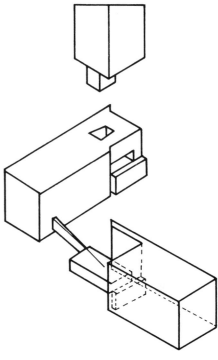

Blind mitered half-housed mortise and tenon with wedge (Sumidome-hozo-sashi)

Dovetailed mortise-
and-tenon joints

The dovetailed mortise and tenon,
which is known in the West but more
popular in Japan, is an excellent tension-resistant corner joint. Uneven
wood shrinkage across and along the
grain works to this joint's advantage,
because the tenon tends to seat more
firmly in the mortise rather than become loose as the wood moves. The
dovetailed mortise and tenon is more
suitable for use as a right-angled joint
than as a splicing joint, because the
mortise is not subject to checking and
shearing. The dovetailed corner joint's
only weak points are on the sides of
the pin.

The **blind mitered dovetail mortise and tenon** provides a very stable
corner joint, especially between members of unequal width. It is a popular
cabinetmaking joint.

The **dovetailed keyhole joint,** or
housed dovetail, corresponds in function to the simple wedged mortise and
tenon, though it is less resistant to
shear stress and bending. The full-
shouldered form of this joint (see the
top drawing at right) is used primarily
on the lower ends of queen posts, to
anchor the roof against strong winds.
In furniture making it provides a secret
knockdown connection.

Blind mitered dovetail mortise and tenon (Handome/Kakushi-ari)

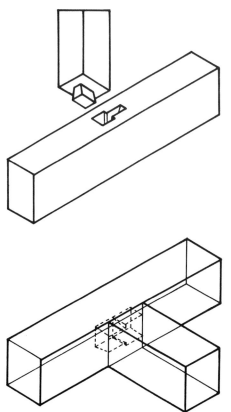

*Dovetailed keyhole joint or housed
dovetail* (Fukuro-ari/Ari-otoshi/
Kama-hozo)

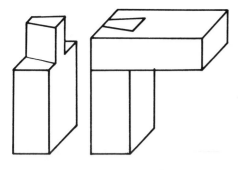

Through single dovetail (Ari-kata-san-mai-hozo)

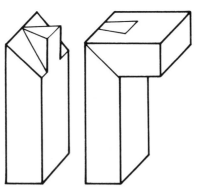

Through mitered single dovetail for frames (Tome-ari-kata-san-mai-hozo)

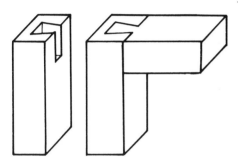

Half-blind single dovetail (Kakushi-ari-kata-san-mai-hozo)

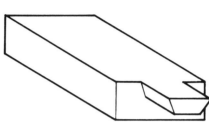

Dovetail tenon (Ari-hozo)

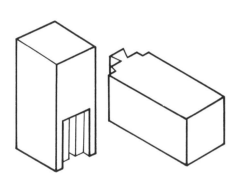

Cogged dovetail for threshold-to-jamb joinery (Eriwa-tsuki-ari-otoshi)

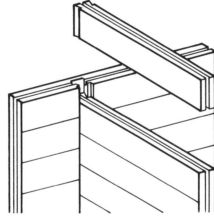

Dovetail for solid-wall framing

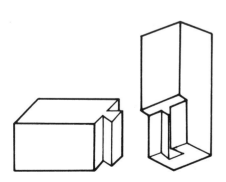

Dovetailed stop lap for threshold-to-jamb joinery (Kageiri-ari-otoshi)

Wedged dovetails

The **wedged half dovetail** is better suited for wall-frame joinery, because the mortised member is weakened less and the joint has greater load-bearing capacity. In this application, the tenon is inserted vertically in the post, not horizontally.

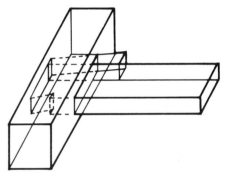

Wedged half dovetail (Shitage-kama)

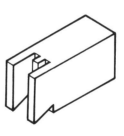

Double half-dovetail tenons with stub tenon for wedged joint (Shitage-kama)

Gooseneck tenons

The use of loose hardwood tenons makes it possible to add new beams between existing posts. The end of the tenon that fits in the post is cut with a dovetail; the opposite end has a gooseneck, or hammerhead, and a slot for a wedge. The load on the cross beam is transferred to the post by a stub tenon under the loose tenon.

The **gooseneck mortise-and-tenon joint** is a relatively rigid joint that is used for framing door openings in log buildings and for assembling Japanese sliding *shoji* panels.

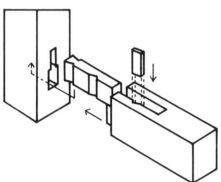

Loose gooseneck/dovetail tenon for wall framing

Gooseneck mortise-and-tenon joint on a chamfered frame (Otoshi-gama)

Gooseneck mortise-and-tenon joint at a sill corner (Kiguchi-ari)

Lap Joints

Like the mortise and tenon, the lap joint has a large number of variations that are derived from a simple, basic form. Lap joints, or halved joints, are as old as mortise-and-tenon joints, and they are used in right-angled joinery as corner laps, T-shaped laps or cross laps.

In basic lap-joint design, the ends of two pieces of wood overlap, or one member crosses another. The main difference between lap joints and cogged joints, which are discussed on pp. 115-119, is that the top surfaces of the mating members are flush in a lap joint. Common construction applications for lap joints are as corner joints for sills and wall plates in framed walls. They are used in interior finish work to join thin boards, such as frieze boards, table pedestals and window mullions.

The cross lap can be made at angles other than 90°, as shown in the photos of the oblique cross lap at right.

As mentioned in the discussion of the lap joint as a splicing joint (see p. 32), horizontal lap joints need support from below if they are to bear loads, because cutting the lap weakens the wood. Gluing the joint does not significantly increase its strength.

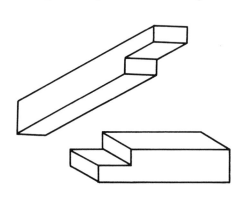

Corner lap

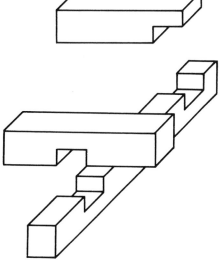

Simple cross lap and T-shaped lap

Oblique cross lap (Naname-ai-gaki-kumi-te)

Blind corner laps and beveled half laps

Like the open mortise and tenon, the **corner lap** can be mitered to conceal the joint and provide better protection against the weather.

The **beveled half lap** (or **French lock joint**) is an easy way to join sills so that they resist tension. The locking effect is achieved by beveling the cheeks of the laps, which are pressed firmly together by the weight of the load on the sills.

The effectiveness of the beveled half lap is somewhat reduced if it is made as a blind joint. The **blind beveled half lap** must be well protected against moisture, so that water does not collect at the low point of the angled lap and cause decay.

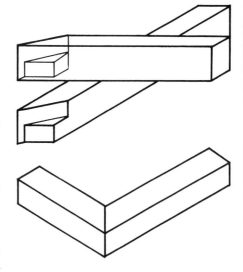

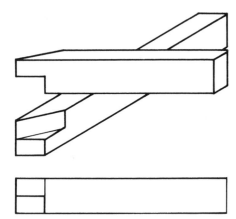

Blind mitered corner lap

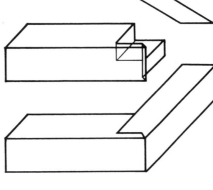

Blind corner lap

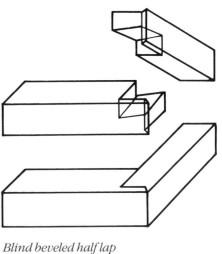

Mitered corner lap

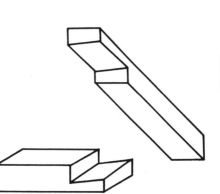

Beveled half lap

Blind beveled half lap

102

Tabled lap joints

The beveled half lap loses its effectiveness if the bearing load on the horizontal beam is too light. In such cases, a somewhat more elaborate **tabled lap joint** should be used to provide resistance to tension.

When the tabled lap is used as a T-shaped joint, the table, or hook, must be long enough to resist shear. If necessary, the beam's end can be extended beyond the edge of the supporting member to increase the length of the table (and shear resistance). The disadvantage of the tabled lap is that it weakens its mating members more than the common lap joint, because more wood is removed.

When the tabled lap is used as a corner joint, the shoulders of the tables must be angled to prevent lateral movement. The **sloped tabled corner lap joint** simplifies wall-plate joinery in timber-frame buildings, because the joint seats itself, eliminating the need for additional means to position members.

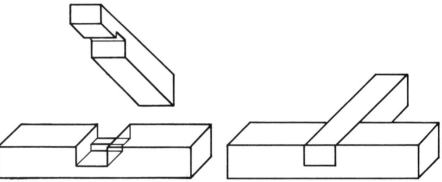

Tabled lap joint

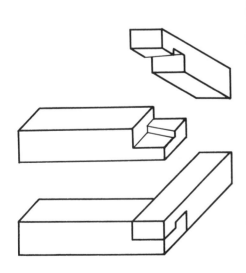

Sloped tabled corner lap joint

As with most blind joints, the stability of the **blind sloped tabled lap joint** is somewhat sacrificed for the sake of appearance and increased protection against the weather.

The **Japanese sloped tabled corner lap** is a suitable joint to use when resistance to lateral movement is more important than resistance to tension. The **tabled lap with dovetail tenon** provides greater resistance to tension and less weakening of the load-bearing member. It is used to connect beams under tension to the wall plates in timber-frame houses. In Japan, the wall plate also functions as the foot purlin and its top outside edge is beveled to receive the rafters (see the drawing at bottom right). The joint is mortised to accept the wall post's tenon from below, which provides additional stability.

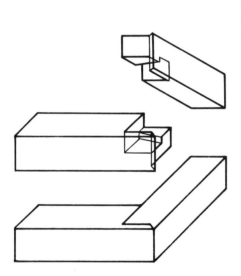

Blind sloped tabled corner lap

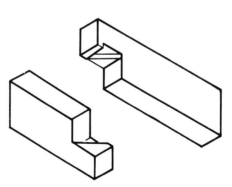

Japanese sloped tabled corner lap

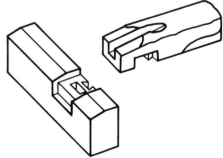

Mortised tabled lap with dovetail tenon (Kabuto-ari)

Another way to increase the tension resistance of a lap joint is to use a **dovetail lap.** The dovetail lap weakens the bearing member less than a tabled lap, but its angular stability is reduced. To ensure a durable dovetail joint, careful wood selection is essential (as explained on p. 42).

Housing the dovetail increases its resistance to lateral shear stress as well as its load-carrying capacity.

Although the **half-dovetail lap** is more commonly used as an oblique joint for connecting roof braces, collar ties and rafters (see p. 79), it can also be used as a right-angled joint for framing openings in floors and ceilings.

The dovetail-lap form can be created by inserting wedges into the end grain of a common lap, as shown in the drawing of the Viennese timber-frame truss at far right.

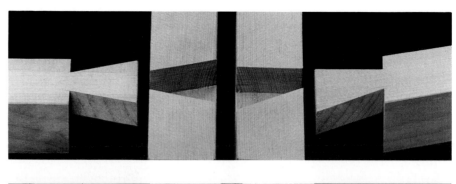

Simple dovetail lap (Tsutsumi-ari-gata-ai-gaki-tsugi)

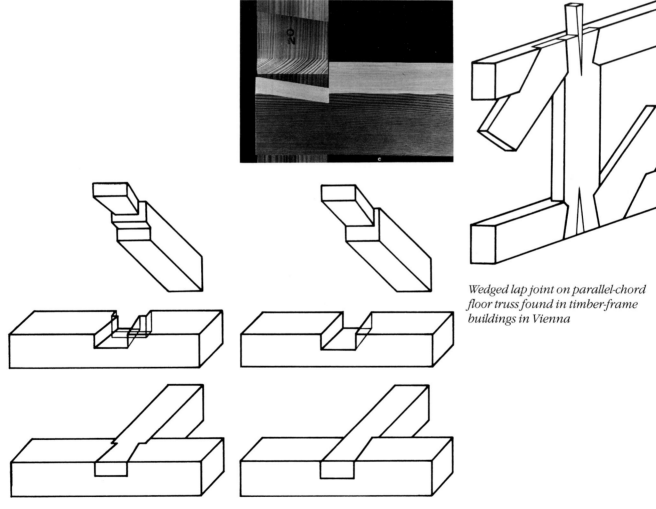

Wedged lap joint on parallel-chord floor truss found in timber-frame buildings in Vienna

Housed dovetail lap

Half-dovetail lap (Naname-ari-ai-gaki-tsugi)

Lap joints in log buildings

Log structures have been built in the wooded areas of both Japan and Europe since the Middle Ages. Log building was particularly well developed in Norway, because the Norwegians under Swedish rule were not permitted to build stone houses.

Log houses require straight, uniform-sized round timbers. By alternately fitting a log's foot end to the top end of the log below, the tree's natural taper was utilized to achieve uniform wall height in early log structures. The development of more sophisticated tools made it possible to dress the logs so that they would fit parallel to each other, which made for houses with tighter walls and better protection against the wind.

The construction of a log house requires an experienced housewright who is familiar with the unique difficulties of this type of building. Because the timbers lie horizontally on top of each other, transverse shrinkage must be taken into account throughout the building process. As the timbers dry, the walls settle and lose height. Problems arise where there are uprights, such as door posts, because the posts shrink much less along their length than do the logs across their width. To allow for the different rates of shrinkage, the joint between the uprights and the end of the horizontal timbers must be movable. This is accomplished by using a sliding open mortise-and-tenon joint. The same consideration must be taken for window frames, chimneys, wall paneling and conduits for plumbing and wiring. Failure to take into account the different rates of shrinkage of horizontal logs and upright posts will cause the joints between the logs to open and the corner joints to break apart.

Depending on the method of construction, corner joints in log structures can differ in the following ways:

1. They can be flush with the walls, or the head of the beam can project beyond the corner.

2. They can be joined with common laps or cross laps, or with more complex cogged joints.

3. The head of the beam at the corner joint can be triangular, square, pentagonal or hexagonal, or oval, round or even rhombic.

Whatever construction method is used, the joints must have a tight fit to prevent wind infiltration.

On corners, **common half laps** must be pinned with hardwood dowels to prevent movement. The **cross lap** is an improvement on the common half lap, because each beam is tied into the beam above and the one below. The **quarter lap** is a solid joint that prevents movement at the corner.

Swiss chalet building is a modern form of log building that uses thick planks instead of logs. The **chalet joint** is offset and rabbeted to provide better protection against wind infiltration. The planks, which are uniform in size and usually grooved, are joined edgewise. The wall is built as a shell with insulation in between.

Tension-resistant joints for log structures can be made by cutting the lap in a trapezoid form, as exemplified by the **offset dovetail lap joint**.

Lapped dovetails used to tie interior walls into outer walls are similar in principle to quarter-lap joints, with the edge cheeks cut at an angle. In the **finger-lap joint,** by contrast, the face cheeks are sloped.

Dovetailed corner lap joints are similar to beveled half laps. Curved, interlocking mating surfaces are the hallmark of the traditional **Klingschrot joint.**

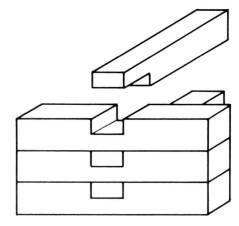

Common T-shaped half lap

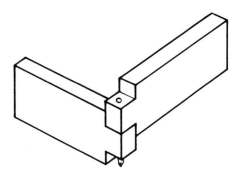

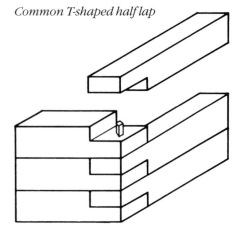

Pinned corner lap

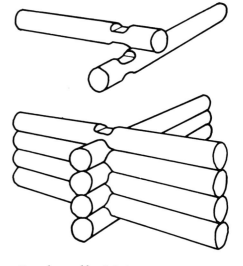

Cross-lapped log joints

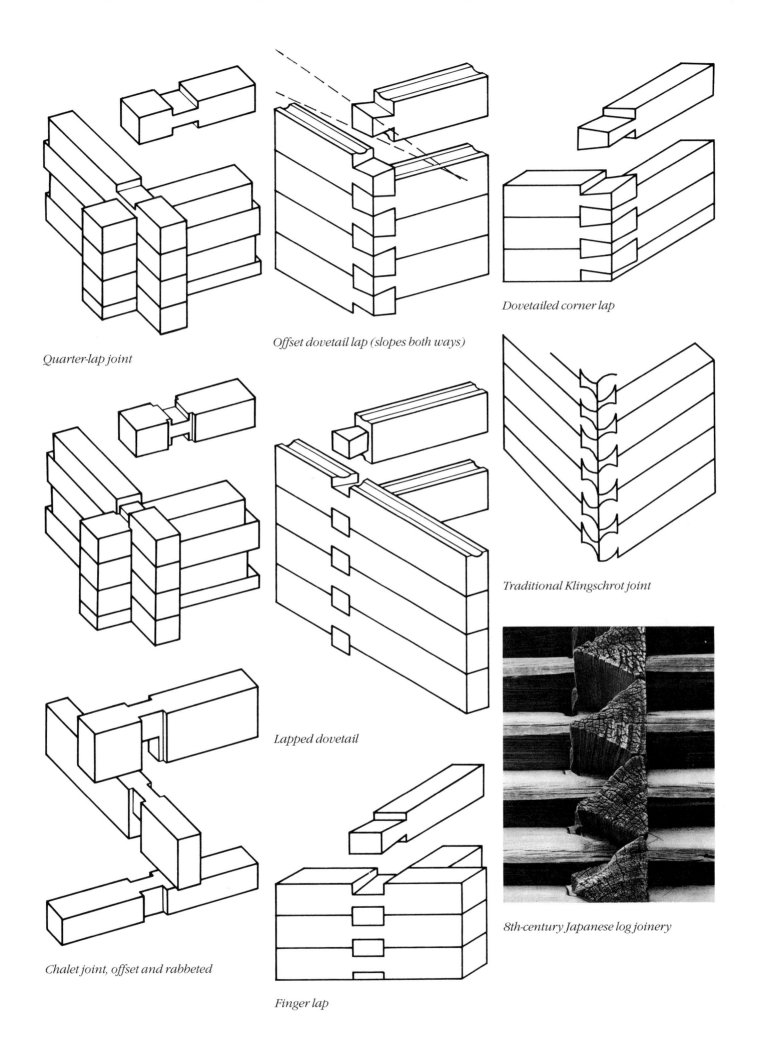

Quarter-lap joint

Offset dovetail lap (slopes both ways)

Dovetailed corner lap

Chalet joint, offset and rabbeted

Lapped dovetail

Traditional Klingschrot joint

Finger lap

8th-century Japanese log joinery

Stop laps

Stop laps are used to form T-shaped joints between joists and beams and beams and sills. The laps do not extend across the full width of the mating member and therefore do not weaken load-bearing beams as much as common lap joints. The disadvantage is that the bearing surfaces of the laps are reduced.

The **simple stop lap** must be pinned if it is used on upright posts. Unpinned, the lap can slide out of its mortise if the bearing member warps or twists.

The **sloped stop lap** weakens the bearing member the least, because it leaves the timber's upper, compression zone almost completely intact.

To minimize the risk of the lap slipping out of the bearing member, a **half-dovetail stop lap** or a **dovetail stop lap** can be used to lock the lap in place.

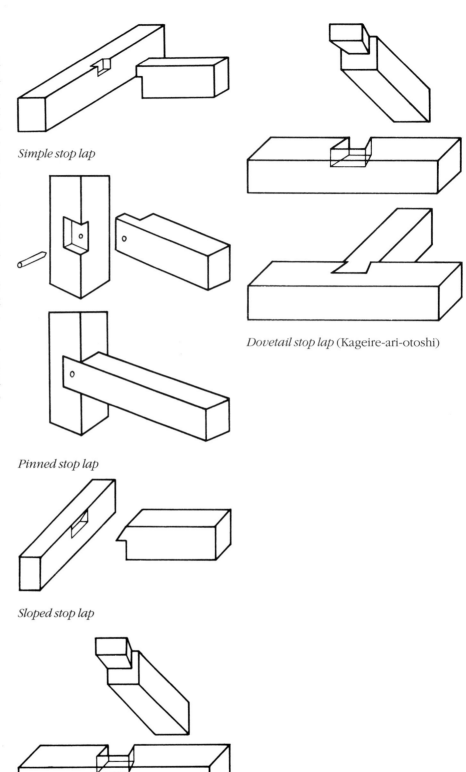

Simple stop lap

Pinned stop lap

Sloped stop lap

Dovetail stop lap (Kageire-ari-otoshi)

Half-dovetail stop lap

The **Japanese housed dovetail stop lap** can withstand stress in all directions. Housing increases the joint's resistance to shear and twisting and also improves its load-bearing capacity. If a mortise for a post's tenon is made at the lap joint, the notch for the dovetail lap is much easier to cut. At the same time, the post prevents the lap from pushing up out of the joint.

In Japanese houses, foot purlins are often joined to the corner posts with dovetail stop laps, which are held in place from below by the post's tenon.

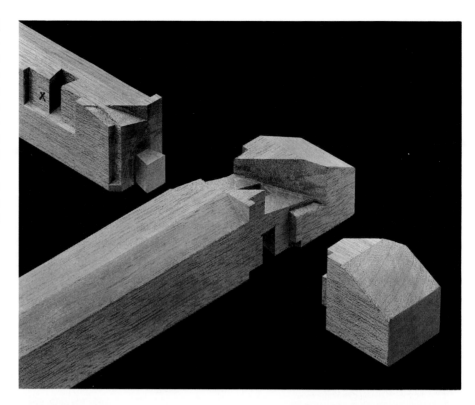

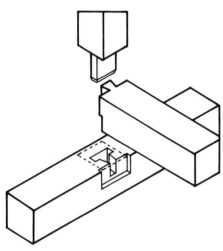

Housed dovetail stop lap with mortise for post's tenon (Ari-kake)

The **blind dovetail stop lap** is used to connect tension beams to the foot purlin, or wall plate. The **blind housed dovetail stop lap** presents a large number of bearing surfaces. This strong, high-quality joint prevents the timbers from twisting and ensures a precise, lasting fit.

Another Japanese joint combining the lap and the dovetail is the **lap joint with sliding dovetail tongues.** The tongues, or feathers, are cut on the underside of the lap to secure the beam to the supporting member. This joint is used to attach floor joists to groundsills.

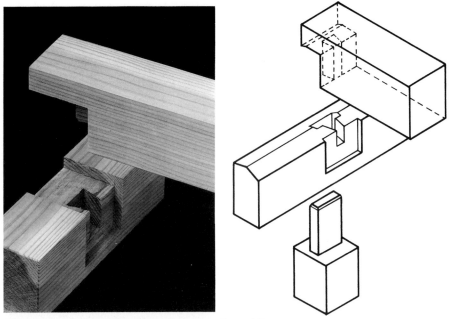

Blind housed dovetail stop lap (Kabuto-ari-otoshi)

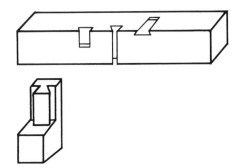

Lap joint with sliding dovetail tongue (Neda-hori)

Blind corner lap with dovetail tongues, for joining eave boards on a hip roof

110

Cross-lap joints

Cross-lap joints, which are superior to common lap joints, can be made in a variety of ways.

The **simple cross lap** is used for horizontal and vertical cross joints in roof trusses, and for cross bracing and diagonal cross bracing in walls. It's also common in frames for upholstered furniture. Because the cross lap weakens its mating members, in modern construction this joint is often replaced by metal fasteners. In this method of construction, the cross joint is formed by bolting two separate beams on either side of an integral timber.

Simple cross laps are not good glue joints, because glued end grain does not adhere well to cross grain. In wall bracing, one solution is to make one solid brace, and instead of cross lapping, mortise in two members at the junction.

On coped window mullions and coped rails and stiles on paneled ceilings, the edges of the crossing bars must be mitered and the lap offset to meet at the narrow part of the miter.

The **V-mitered cross lap** increases the area of the side mating surfaces, thereby ensuring greater resistance to twisting. Mitered cross-lap joints can be glued.

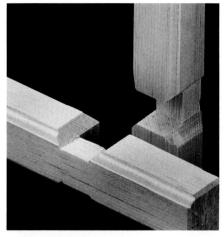

Offset mitered cross lap (Go-ten-jyo-gata)

V-mitered cross lap (Ken-saki-dome-ai-gaki-tsugi)

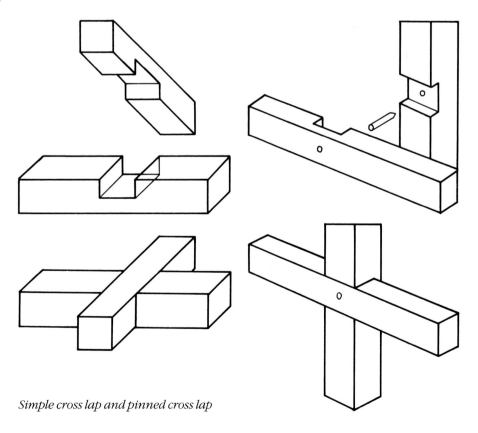

Simple cross lap and pinned cross lap

Glazing bars in framed doors and windows can be joined with various forms of the cross lap. To obtain clean miters it is common to cross-lap just the ribbing, then cover it with a fillister molding. (The fillister is the rebate that receives the glass.) When more than two glazing bars meet at a junction, they should be joined with a spline rather than a cross lap to increase the gluing surface.

The possibility of the joint opening, which is a problem with the simple cross lap, is eliminated with the **offset cross lap**. The larger mating surface gives it greater stability. The disadvantage of the offset cross lap is that it can be used only for structures that carry light loads or are supported from below. A variation of this joint is the **double offset cross lap,** which ensures a lasting, precise fit.

The **tabled cross lap** weakens the supporting timber less than the simple cross lap, and the joint cannot shift. The **dovetailed cross lap** is a more complex joint to make, but it combines all the advantages of the above-mentioned cross laps and also creates a decorative effect.

In Japan, the head of the gable-end foot purlin is sometimes joined to the longitudinal wall plate beyond the corner post. A dovetail tenon on the extension piece slides into the wall plate from below. This makes it unnecessary to cut a cross lap, which would weaken the load-bearing plate too much.

The offset cross lap can be reinforced with a post's through tenon, which must be haunched so that the underlying member is not weakened too much in section. This form of the cross lap is often used as a sill corner joint in Japan.

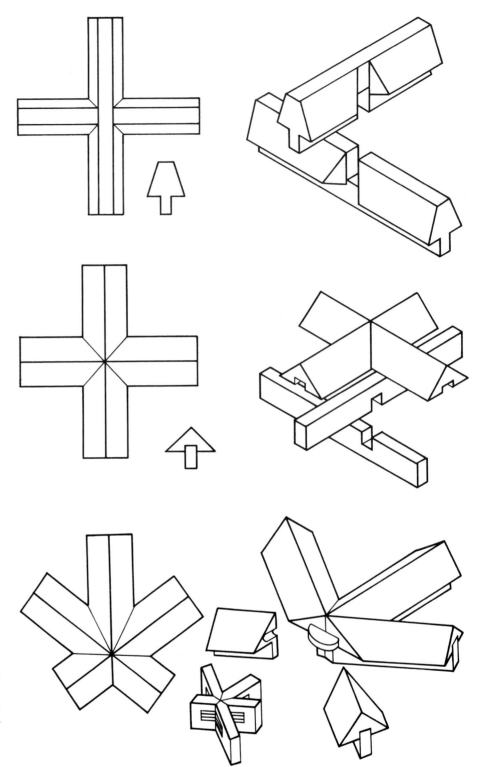

Cross-lapped and splined glazing bars

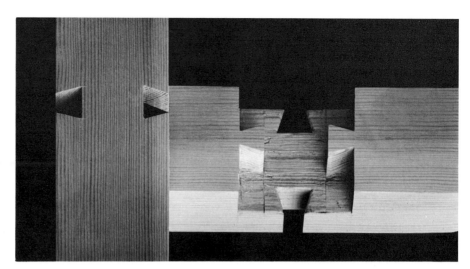

Dovetailed cross lap
(Shi-ho-ari-kumi-te)

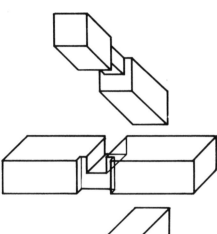

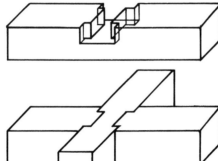

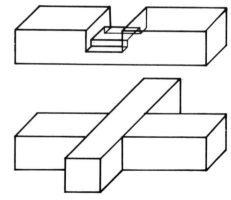

Offset cross lap

Double offset cross lap

Tabled cross lap

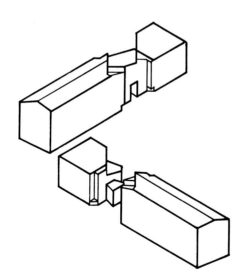

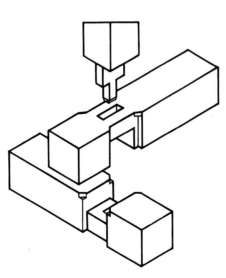

Japanese foot-purlin joint

*Offset and housed cross lap with
haunched through tenon*

Cross-lapped purlins and bracket construction

During the 12th century, Chinese missionaries spread Buddhism to Japan, supplanting Shintoism, the traditional Japanese religion. In the wake of this conversion, numerous Buddhist temples were constructed in the traditional Chinese building style. Hitherto unknown construction elements appeared in Japan, such as richly ornamented projecting purlin heads and complex bracket joints under the roof overhang. The large number of joints required to tie the elements together provided the elasticity necessary to withstand the tremors of earthquakes.

Projecting purlin heads make it possible to cross-lap the corner joint, with pins and dovetail tenons for reinforcement, which provides better protection against shifting.

The multipartite brackets and cornices require a variety of joint forms, among them cross laps and cogged joints.

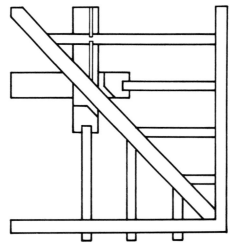

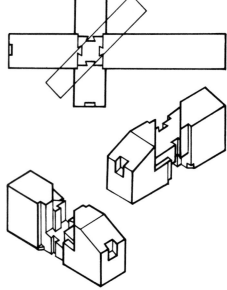

Plan view of a Japanese roof truss with cross-lapped foot purlins, hip rafter and jack rafters

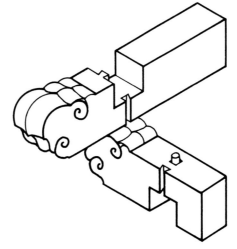

Cross-lapped foot-purlin corner joints

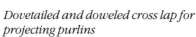

Dovetailed and doweled cross lap for projecting purlins

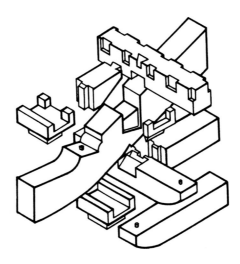

Bracket complex with cross laps and cogged joints

Cogged Joints

Cogged joints differ from common lap joints in that the surfaces of the cogged members are not flush and the members are always horizontal. An exception is found in the trusses of some engineered structures, though here the cogged joints must always be secured with bolts.

The advantage of the cogged joint is that it does not significantly weaken the cogged timbers, because the cog is only 2 cm (¾ in.) deep.

Cog joints are used to connect floor joists to sills and ceiling joists to plates, as corner joints on purlins, and on bridging between purlins. In multi-storied structures, they are used to tie floor joists to wall plates.

The floor structure often has to transfer horizontal forces of tension and compression between the plates or sills of facing walls. It must tie the exterior and interior walls together and provide the necessary resistance to withstand stress from the wind. Cogged joints enhance a structure's rigidity and, if carefully executed, prevent timbers from twisting or tilting.

Cogged joints have small lateral mating surfaces. They must therefore seat well on the horizontal mating surfaces so the upper timber does not teeter. The cog should be designed so that the bottom edge of the upper timber—at least in part—has its full width resting on the lower member. For example, a simple cog should never be used under a plate or purlin, and a dovetailed cog should not be used under a floor joist or beam.

The long-term stability of cogged joints can be threatened by checks that appear in the end grain of the cogged beam. The best way to overcome this

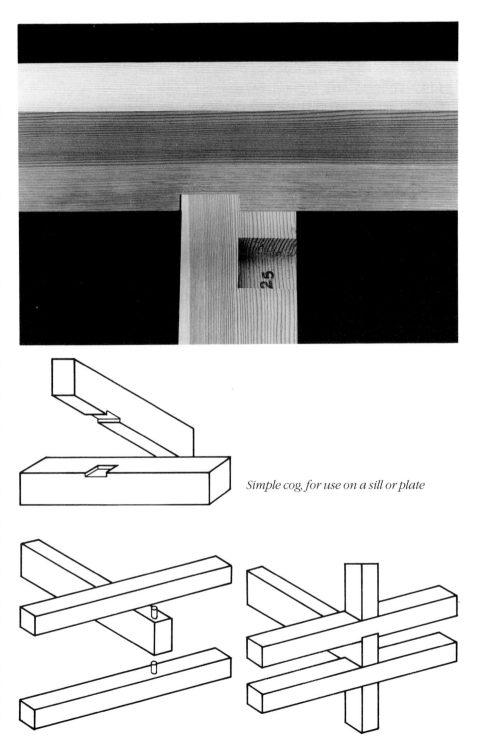

Simple cog, for use on a sill or plate

Doweled cogged joint

problem is to extend the beam's end about 10 cm (4 in.) beyond the edge of the supporting timber. Cogged timbers should always be loaded from above, and they can be reinforced with dowels or treenails. The dowels are usually about 11 cm (4½ in.) long and 3 cm (1¼ in.) in diameter, with beveled end-edges.

Those who are against the use of cogged joints maintain that these joints were originally used exclusively to adjust the height of irregular timbers to the same elevation. With today's standard-dimension timbers, they argue, cogs can be effectively replaced by dowels, lowering construction costs. This argument is valid when considering forces of tension, because the shear surface of a dowel is about twice as great as that of the cross cog and equal to that of the simple cog. The reverse is true, however, for resistance to compression: The cross cog can withstand twice as much compression load as the dowel, and the simple cog only 20% less than the dowel. Hence, the dowel is cost-effective only when resistance to tension is paramount.

The **simple cogged joint** is used only on sills under the floor framework. Groundsills in timber-framed walls tend to teeter under the weight of the wall if supported only with simple cogs.

The timber-frame construction method with floors overhanging each other has proven to be effective. The weight of the upper stories on the bearing point of the wall below is transferred toward the outside through the ends of the floor and ceiling beams. Under the weight of the timber-frame wall, the ends of the beams bend slightly downward. Like a seesaw, the part of the framework inside the building is bowed slightly upward, which, according to the principle of pre-tensioned beams, increases the load-carrying capacity of the floor framework.

The **double cogged joint** is used as a cross joint for continuous wall timbers. The **cross cogged joint** can be used under or over a floor or ceiling framework, but the end of the upper timber should always extend at least 10 cm (4 in.) beyond the edge of the beam below to prevent splitting of the end grain.

The **dovetail cog** should only be used on the top side of a framing beam so that the beam does not tilt.

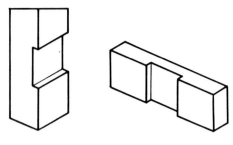

Simple Japanese cog

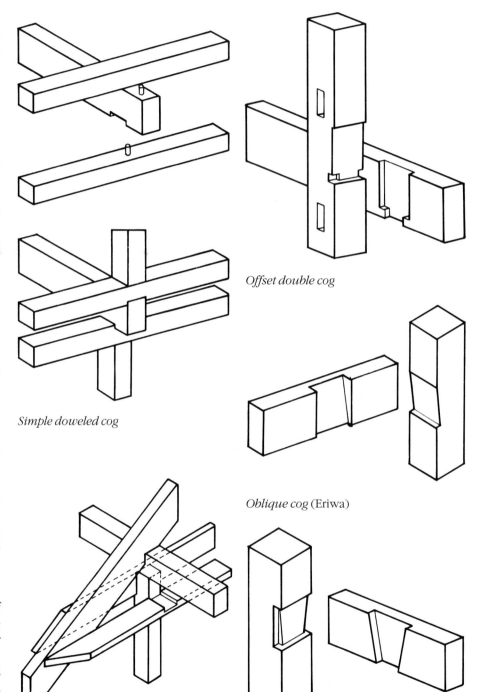

Simple doweled cog

Simple cog at the eaves in European construction

Offset double cog

Oblique cog (Eriwa)

Housed dovetail cog

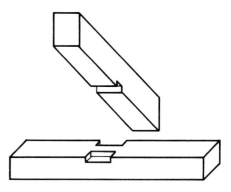

Double cog (Watari-ago)

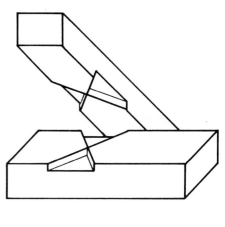

Cross cog (Tasuki-kake-watari-ago)

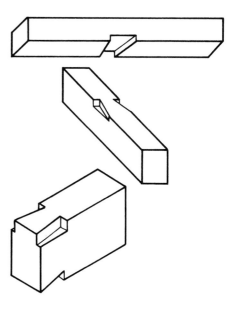

Dovetail cog

The **half-cross corner cog** prevents the upper timber from sliding off the supporting member's end at the corner. The **oblique corner cog** and the **half-dovetail corner cog** serve the same purpose.

Some Japanese variations of the cogged joint are shown on the facing page. Of particular interest is the joint between the hip rafter and the foot purlin. The hip rafter is joined over the purlin corner with a cog-like bird's mouth, and the corner is reinforced by the haunched tenon of the supporting post. The hip rafter is attached to the ridge purlin with a tension joint, which relieves stress on the corner joint.

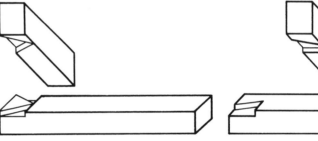

Half-cross corner cog

Oblique corner cog

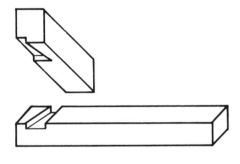

Half-dovetail corner cog

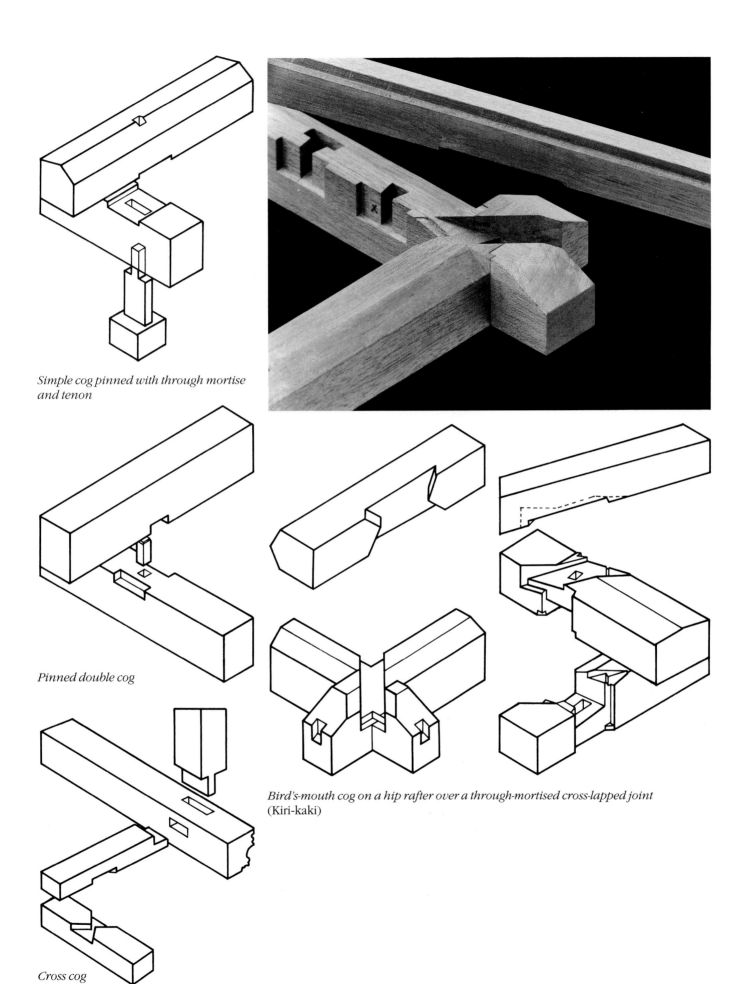

Simple cog pinned with through mortise
and tenon

Pinned double cog

Cross cog

Bird's-mouth cog on a hip rafter over a through-mortised cross-lapped joint
(Kiri-kaki)

Tongue Joints

In Japan, tongue joints play an important role in right-angled joinery. Their main function is to prevent beams from twisting, though in light floor and ceiling framing they are sometimes the sole means of support.

Sills can be joined at the corner with a **blind mitered double tongue joint.** The corner post with fan-shaped tenon locks and covers the joint. The mating parts of the joint must be assembled vertically.

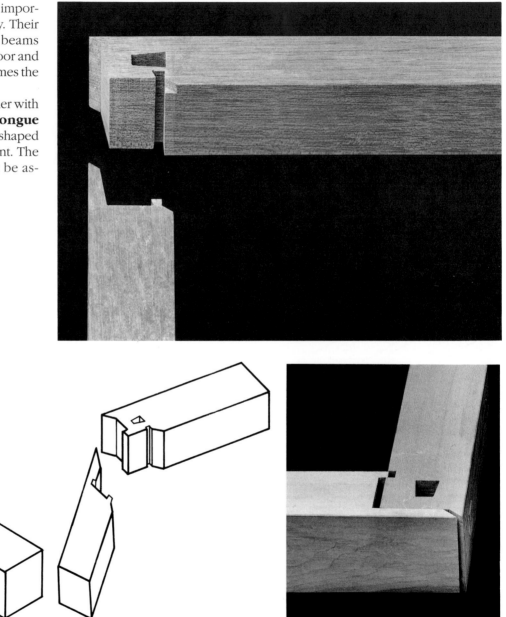

Blind mitered tongue joints, mortised for corner posts

Other uses for right-angled tongue joints are on door casings and thresholds, sliding door channels, and light framing between wall posts.

The **oblique tongue joint** is sometimes used to attach barge boards to the ends of purlins on the gable end of a house.

Purlin end cut for joint with cornice beam

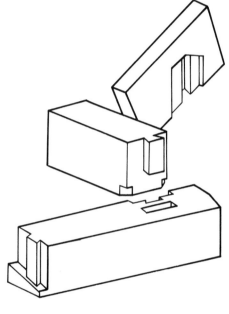

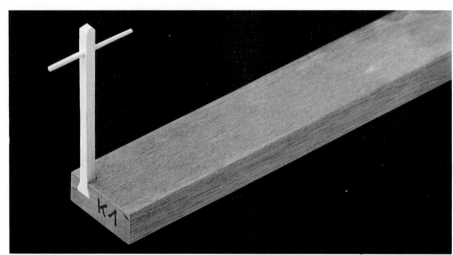

Loose tongue for a light timber

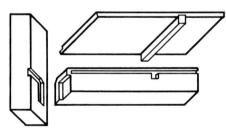

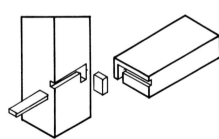

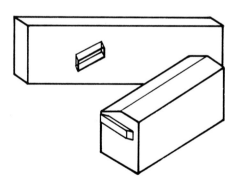

Oblique tongue joints (Shakushi-hozo)

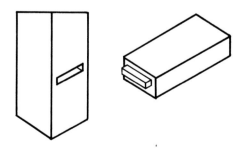

Straight tongue joints

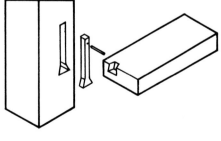

Loose tongue joints

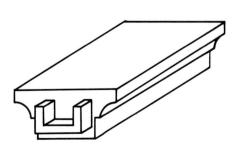

Blind U-shaped tongue
(Hako-mechi-gai-tsugi)

Halved mitered lapped scarf

4 Edge Joints

Edge joints are used to join boards edge to edge or, as in carcase construction, at right angles. Also within this category are joints that are made by inserting sliding battens perpendicular to flat boards to prevent warp. Because the boards that are joined are often wide, it is important to take into account the different rates of shrinkage along and across the grain, especially if the joints are glued. In cabinetmaking long grain cannot be glued to cross grain, because of the risk of the joint tearing apart as the wood shrinks.

There are various ways to prevent racking in edge-joined boards and to prevent the edge joint between the boards from opening. It is important to distinguish between joints that are glued and those that are not. The latter require a solid substructure or a frame to hold the boards together.

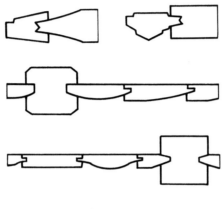

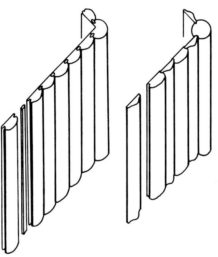

Tongue-and-groove joints in Norwegian plank-wall construction

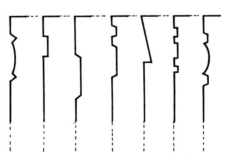

Decorative grooves on timbers in medieval buildings (along the grain)

Rabbeted and Grooved Joints

The **rabbeted joint** (or **ship-lap joint**) is a simple, stable joint for edge-joining boards and paneling. Some of the applications for this joint are on cabinet backs (with the ends of the individual boards housed in grooves in the frame), door panels and floorboards. Because the boards can move within their frames, wood shrinkage does not cause openings to appear between the boards.

The **tongue-and-groove joint** is a very old edge joint that has a multitude of applications, whether as a glued joint or unglued. The earliest tongue-and-groove joints were made with simple splitting tools and drawknives. They were used in the first palisade structures to make board walls airtight and to fit door posts in their openings. In log buildings, the grooves were stuffed with moss to keep the wind out.

In frame construction, wall planks are slid into a grooved frame. In the past, the last three planks were usually tapered and pounded into the groove, which made the wall tight and rigid. This same method of construction was used until recently in Swiss timber-frame houses to prevent the joints between floorboards from opening. The last tapered board projected through the wall on one side, and could be driven in at any time to tighten up the floor.

Grooves were also used as decorative elements, and many different profiles were developed, as shown in the examples from the Middle Ages in the bottom drawing at left.

Tongue-and-groove joints are found in plank construction, flooring, wall paneling and frame-and-panel construction. Today, commercially sawn tongue-and-groove lumber is used extensively for floors and interior finishing.

The modern tongue and groove is the simplest joint for joining boards edge to edge. The tongue should be about one-third the thickness of the board. The groove's cheeks are the weak points of the joint. For a snug fit on the visible side of the joint, the back cheek should be somewhat narrower than the front cheek. On tongue-and-groove flooring, the upper cheek should be thicker than the lower one so that it does not break under the load on the floor.

The **spline-and-groove joint,** or **loose spline,** was already known in Roman times and was used in the plank ceilings of Romanesque stone churches. One advantage of the splined joint is that it saves wood; another is that it saves time for the craftsman, because it is not necessary to cut two different profiles on the edges of the boards to be joined. Today, splines are made of plywood or of cross-grain hardwood or softwood (with the grain running perpendicular to the groove).

It is not advisable to use splines with longitudinal grain, because they split easily. Commercially, splines are used in parquet flooring and in paneling. **Double splines** on thick boards provide added resistance to twist.

Rabbeted joint (front), tongue and groove (middle) and spline and groove (back) (Ai-gaki-tsugi/Hon-zane-tsugi/Yatoi-zane-tsugi)

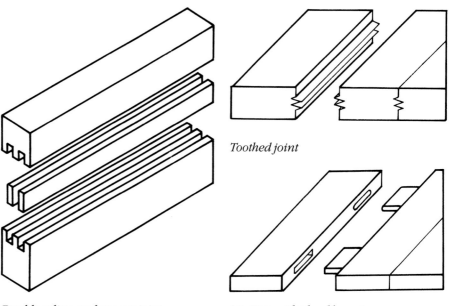

Toothed joint

Double spline-and-groove joint

Mortises with glued loose tenons

The Japanese **dovetail tongue-and-groove joint** is little known in the West. Compared to the common tongue and groove, this joint is more prone to shear failure, but it does keep the joint from opening and resists shift. The dovetail tongue and groove is suitable for edge-joining wood that is otherwise difficult to glue, such as green oak or padauk. It is also used on surfaces exposed to the weather.

In other cases, edge joints must be glued, as on certain types of floors and side partitions. Here, the joints to use include the tongue and groove, the rabbeted joint, the **doweled joint** (see the photo at right) or the machined **toothed joint** (see the top right drawing on p. 125). It is essential to choose the correct method of gluing and to take into account the different rates of wood shrinkage. The **mortise with loose tenon joint** (see the bottom right drawing on p. 125) is a solid and relatively easy joint to make for workbenches, heavy-duty work tables and leafed tables. It is a strong joint even if not glued.

For the cabinetmaker, rabbeted and tongue-and-groove joints have a wider range of application as right-angled joints than as edge-to-edge joints. Rabbeted joints are durable glue joints for cabinet carcases. They are easy to assemble and do not slip as the glue sets up. Tongue-and-groove joints are used for cabinet backs, drawer partitions and drawer bottoms. Today, most grooved frames are made of solid wood and the housed panels are of plywood, sometimes glued and sometimes not.

Doweled joint and dovetail tongue and groove (Da-bo-tsugi/Ari-tsugi)

Blind dovetail tongue and groove (Kakushi-ari-tsugi)

End-grain edging

End-grain edging hides the end grain, which makes finish work easier and provides a solid surface for mounting hardware. It also helps to keep boards flat. To withstand the stress caused by wood shrinkage, the edging should be of fairly wide and very dry hardwood. On very wide boards, dimensional change across the width of the board caused by wood movement is too great to allow use of end-grain edging. In such cases the dovetail batten (discussed on pp. 133-134) is a more effective device for keeping the board surfaces flat.

Because end-grain edging is a joint between long grain and cross grain, it should be glued, wedged or otherwise fastened only close to the center of the board. **Tongue-and-groove edging,** which is used only on narrow boards, is glued in the middle of the joint so that it does not come apart. **Tongue-and-groove edging with a wedged mortise and tenon** is suitable for use on wider boards. Doors and table leaves on quality furniture, such as Baroque and Biedermeier-style, are sometimes edged with **glued splines.** This technique is most common on veneered furniture whose edges and surfaces are polished. **Glued V-edging** creates clean edges on veneered plywood.

Mitered tongue-and-groove edging makes an elegant and solid edge on high-quality furniture. The joint should be glued only at the miter, which should be cut on only one end of the edging to prevent joint failure caused by shrinkage of the board. Mitered tongue-and-groove edging is particularly well suited for use on doors whose hinge side is hidden, as on the fall flap of a secretary.

Offset mitered tongue-and-groove edging (Hon-zane-dome-hashi-bame)

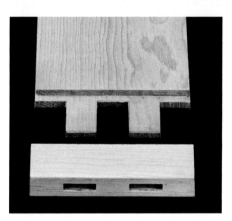

Double-tenoned tongued edging (Hon-zane-toshi-hozo-hashi-bame-tsugi)

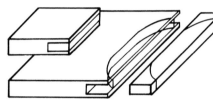

Glued edge spline

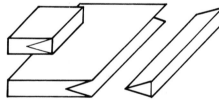

Glued V-edging

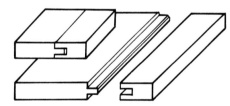

Tongue-and-groove edging

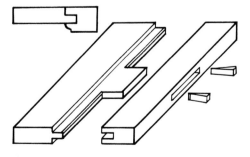

Tongue-and-groove edging with wedged mortise and tenon

Frame-and-panel construction

Enclosing a movable panel in a frame makes it possible to construct large wood surfaces whose overall dimensions do not change significantly as the wood shrinks and swells. In addition, a solid frame keeps the panel from warping. Frame-and-panel construction is especially important for making high-quality furniture and doors.

Panels on simple furniture are housed in grooves in a thicker frame. In this application, the frame and panel usually do not form a flush surface, because the panel thickness matches the width of the groove in the frame. The individual boards of the panel are set in the groove of the frame in such a way that they cannot warp yet can still move freely laterally as the wood shrinks and swells.

Panels can also be installed in rabbeted frames and secured with moldings, as shown in the bottom drawing at right. Frames on high-quality furniture are often mitered and beaded, as shown in the drawing at far right.

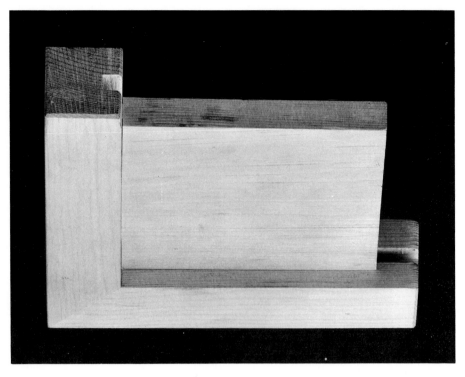

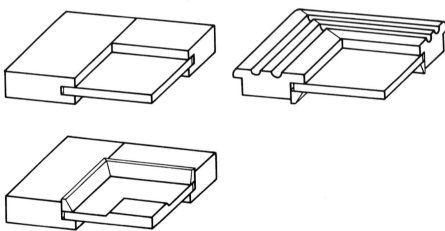

Grooved and rabbeted frames in frame-and-panel construction

Lap Joints

Lengthening boards by means of a **mitered lapped scarf joint** is a technique little known in the West. The large gluing surfaces ensure a strong joint.

The **halved mitered lapped scarf** is a more resilient version of this joint. The symmetrical mating surfaces provide the increased strength and also ensure better resistance against twisting. In addition, the joint wastes less wood because the laps are about half the length of those in the preceding joint. However, these advantages must be weighed against the additional work required to make the joint.

Because the halved mitered lap is relatively inconspicuous, it is a good joint to use for furniture repair.

Mitered lapped scarf (Saba-tsuki-awase-tsugi)

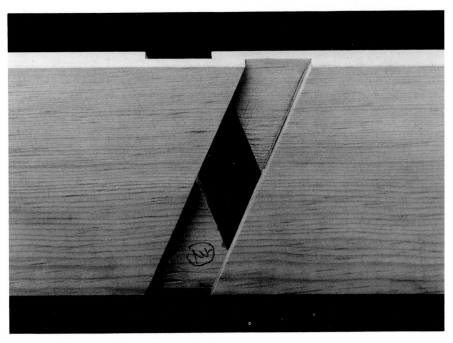

Halved mitered lapped scarf (Ko-sa-saba-tsuki-awase-tsugi)

Carcase Joinery

Edge joints are used in carcase construction to join wide boards at right angles. As a rule, the boards are joined with parallel grain direction, and the joints can be glued. Only a few construction methods require wood to be joined perpendicular to the grain, as when a panel is enclosed in a frame or a dovetail batten is used across a wide board.

Example 1 at right shows the correct way to make a corner joint. Any wood movement will be the same in both boards. In Example 2, unequal wood shrinkage across the two boards will lead to opening of the joint, splitting and uneven edges (circled).

The **half-blind rabbet** is a better corner joint than the simple butt joint because it adds rigidity to the carcase.

The **fully housed dado** is used to increase the load-carrying capacity of shelves. The depth of the dado is usually about one-quarter the thickness of the side panel. The dado joint is not a good joint to use for exposed joinery, however, because it may open as the wood shrinks or cups.

The **sliding dovetail** (see the top right drawing on the facing page) is an excellent tension-resistant joint for joining boards at right angles. It does not require fastening with nails or screws. Because the joint does not open as the boards shrink, the sliding dovetail is often used in high-quality furniture.

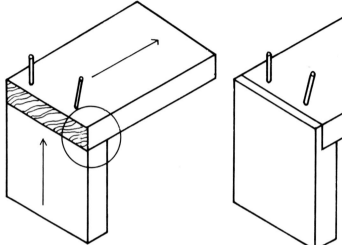

Doweled butt joint with parallel grain (Example 1)

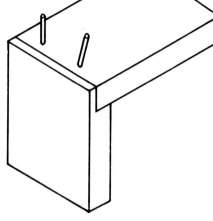

Doweled half-blind rabbet joint

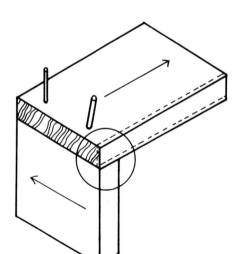

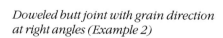

Doweled butt joint with grain direction at right angles (Example 2)

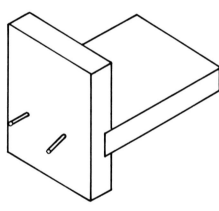

Doweled fully housed dado joint

Tongue-and-dado joints are popular corner joints for carcase furniture, shelving, door casings and drawers. Whether simple, half blind or mitered, these joints are easy to make by machine. An additional advantage is that the boards do not shift during glue-up. Because the lip of the grooved board is the weak point on a corner joint, the tongue must fit precisely. If the fit is too tight, the lip may break when the joint is assembled. If the grooved board is less than 20 mm (¾ in.) thick, it's a good idea to extend the board slightly beyond the corner to strengthen the joint. A small chamfer on the tongue makes the joint easier to assemble.

If the tongue is cut on the upper part of a shelf or drawer bottom, there is a risk that the board will split below the tongue when it is carrying a heavy load. Cutting the tongue on the bottom edge of the board (see the drawing below) strengthens the joint, though it can open slightly on the top side.

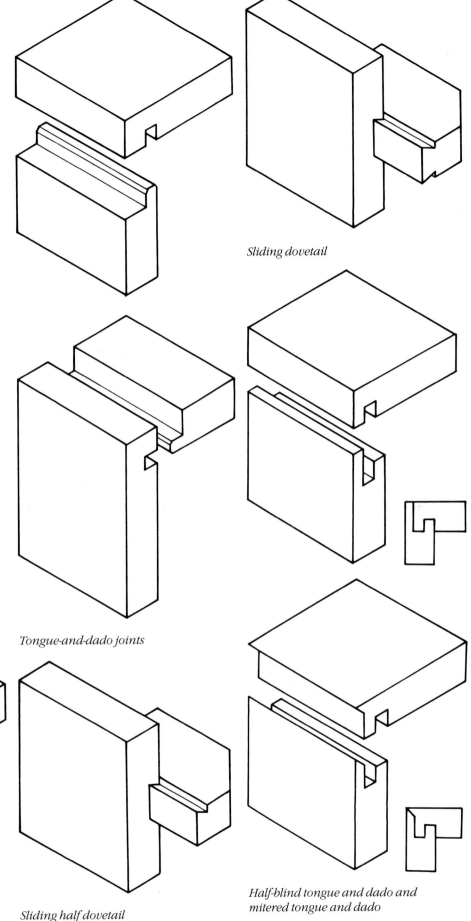

Sliding dovetail

Tongue-and-dado joints

Tongue-and-dado joint for a shelf or drawer bottom

Sliding half dovetail

Half-blind tongue and dado and mitered tongue and dado

Sliding dovetails can be single-shouldered (sliding half dovetail) or double-shouldered (sliding full dovetail). One application for the sliding half dovetail is to join shelves to side partitions when the two parts have parallel grain (which ensures even wood movement). If possible, the single shoulder should be toward the upper surface to conceal sag in the horizontal board. The mating boards can be glued.

The double-shouldered sliding dovetail is an excellent joint for cabinets, drawers and small boxes. To avoid an unsightly gap or protrusion at the edge of the mating boards as a result of unequal wood movement, the dovetail can be stopped just short of the edge and lippings can be glued on the grooved piece. You can save yourself some work by gluing the outer two boards last; it's then possible to groove the central part of the flat surface, which will receive the sliding dovetails, across its entire width.

Left: Fully housed dado joint (O-ire-tsugi)
Right: Sliding dovetail (Ari-gata-o-ire-tsugi)

Left: Doweled half-blind rabbet (Tsutsumi-uchi-tsuki-tsugi)
Right: Tongue and dado (Hon-zane-hako-gata)

Dovetail Battens

Housed **dovetail battens** (also known as **sliding dovetails**) are suitable for joining wood perpendicular to the grain. In furniture making, the dovetail batten is a reliable device for preventing warp in wide wooden surfaces, such as drawer bottoms, partitions, chair seats and table tops.

The dovetail batten slides into mating grooves cut across the grain on the surface of the boards to be joined. The batten holds the individual boards together to form a wide, level surface.

The sliding batten should not be locked in position with screws or adhesives, or longitudinal cracks will appear on the surface of the boards as the wood swells and shrinks with fluctuations in humidity.

The batten should be stopped short of the edge of the board surface so that it does not protrude beyond the edge when the boards shrink across the grain. In addition, the groove on the underside of the board is usually stopped 10 mm (⅜ in.) short of the edge so that it is not visible from the side. The groove can be tapered slightly toward one end to allow the batten to seat more solidly. However, the dovetail batten should fit tightly only along a third of its length and be able to slide easily along the remaining two-thirds.

The groove should be slightly deeper than the dovetail, and the bottom of the groove cut cleanly, so that the batten can slide freely. To avoid weakening the batten, the dovetail should be no more than one-third the thickness of the batten. The dovetail should be cut at an angle of approximately 75°. The batten can also be made with one shoulder, to prevent shelves and drawer bottoms from sagging. If cross grain is joined to cross grain, the batten can be glued along its entire length.

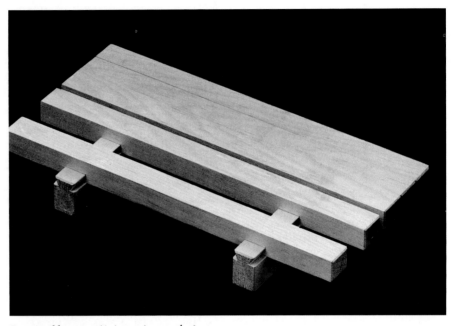

Dovetail battens (Ari-tsugi-suno-ho)

Blind keyhole batten (Kakushi-ari-o-ire-tsugi)

Although the simple dovetail batten is widely used in Western furniture making, in Japan it is more important as a construction joint. On floors and ceilings, boards are often slipped onto dovetailed joists. Dovetailed battens are used on board doors and shutters.

As the keyhole joint shown in the bottom photo on p. 133 illustrates, the sliding batten is not always made with a continuous dovetail. In this way, the joint between the board and the batten is fixed in one lateral direction. In addition, the joint is easy to assemble or dismantle because the dovetail does not have to be slid across the full width of the board.

A further refinement is to compose the dovetail batten of a number of short sections, instead of one continuous piece. The groove is made in the usual way. The short lengths are slid into the groove, and then a grooved cover strip is glued over them. The advantage of this method is that the short batten pieces can be cut from cross grain, which creates a more stable joint.

Square keys or wood bolts can be inserted at right angles through grooves in the batten to lock the batten in place and prevent the boards from shifting sideways, as shown in the photo at right.

Dovetail batten locked with square wood bolts (Kougai-sen-tsugi)

Finger Joints and Dovetails

Finger joints in furniture call to mind the corner joints used in log structures, which, in turn, were perhaps inspired by the interlocking movements of the human hand. Because of their excellent stability, the various forms of finger joints (also known as box joints) are virtually indispensable in the manufacture of drawers and other boxed constructions.

Simple finger joints can be enhanced by pinning them with dowels, which prevent the joint from opening. The dowels are inserted through the outer fingers into the end grain of the mating board.

Multiple finger joints increase the area of the long-grain mating surfaces, which is the ideal gluing situation. The increase in end-grain surfaces is of secondary importance in glue joints, because end grain does not provide a good gluing surface. Multiple finger joints are used on furniture parts subjected to stress, such as furniture bases, carcase corners, game tables and school furniture. Because they can be made easily by machines, finger joints are often used on mass-produced furniture.

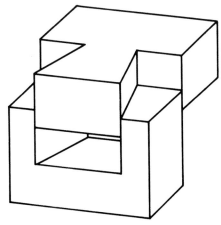

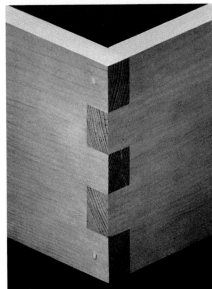

Simple through dovetail

Finger joints: simple (San-mai-hozo-hako-gata), *multiple* (Go-mai-hozo-hako-gata) *and dovetail* (Nana-mai-hozo-hako-gata)

The **dovetail finger joint,** or **drawer dovetail,** is a strong and attractive joint. Even without glue, the joint is resistant to tension in one direction, and it can be secured in the other direction with the aid of dowels. The dovetail gives exceptional stability to hand-made furniture and, like the sliding dovetail, prevents surface twisting. It is often used to join drawer fronts to their sides. The angle of the tails and their mating pins determines the strength of the joint. A ratio of 1:6 is standard.

Usually the tails are made first, then the pins are scribed from the tails. The following formula is often used to calculate the width of the tails:

$$\frac{\text{board's width}}{\text{no. of pins} \times 3 + 1} = \begin{array}{l}\text{tail width at}\\ \text{its midpoint}\end{array}$$

The number of pins is calculated as follows:

$$\frac{\text{board's width}}{1\frac{1}{2} \times \text{board's thickness}}$$

Dovetails should only be cut along the grain.

The finger joint can also be used as a splicing joint. It is simple to make, but is not as good a tension joint as the dovetailed version (see the photos at right). Machine-made tapered finger joints are considerably stronger than straight-sided finger joints.

Finger joint and through dovetail
(Jyu-roku-mai-ari-hako-gata-dome/Nana-mai-ari-hako-gata)

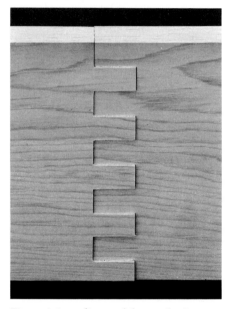

Finger-joint splice and dovetail splice (Jyu-mai-hozo-tsugi/Aari-hozo-tsugi)

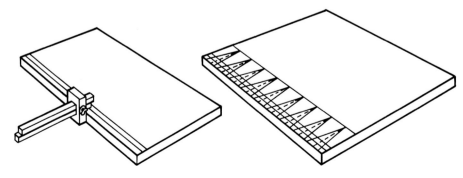

Dovetail layout with a marking gauge: Parallel lines from the board's edge are spaced as follows: line 1, ½ x board thickness; line 2, 1 x board thickness; and line 3, 3 x board thickness. Then, equal-sized, equidistant tails are marked out.

Blind and half-blind dovetails

Dovetail joints can be concealed on one side **(half-blind dovetail)** or two sides **(blind dovetail)**. A **full-blind dovetail** can be made by offsetting the pins and tails and running a miter around all four sides (as shown in the drawing at right).

Blind dovetails are used mainly on decorative boxes, cabinet sides and drawers when it is undesirable to expose the joints.

Among cabinetmakers and carpenters, there are two opposing schools of thought about how to increase a workpiece's aesthetic value. Traditionally, craftsman took great pains to conceal joinery and devised a large number of blind miter joints for this purpose. Yet these joints were no stronger, and often were weaker, than their exposed counterparts.

The effort of the traditional craftsman was rooted in respect, indeed reverence, for the material, wood. It was thought that any evidence of the craftsman's intervention should be as discreet as possible.

With the advent of commercially produced furniture, however, visibly solid and cleanly made joinery became the cabinetmaker's mark of distinction. The workpiece bore the burden of human labor. The introduction of prefabricated houses had a similar effect on the carpenter's relation to his work.

Today, there is a need to expose the joinery as a mark of quality and to develop joinery for decorative purposes.

Half-blind dovetail (Kakushi-ari-hako-gata) *and blind dovetail with mitered corner* (Kakushi-ari-hako-dome)

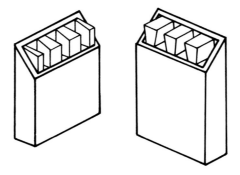

Full-blind mitered dovetail

Decorative dovetail joints

If corner dovetails are to serve as decorative elements, the pins and tails must be in proportion to the thickness of the boards and the size of the furniture. The usual proportions of pins to tails are 1:2, 1:1.5 and 1:1. The equal proportion, 1:1, is the most commonly used in softwood. The widest part of the pins should be one-quarter to one-third the thickness of the board; the half pins at the edges of the board are half dovetails, but they are not half the width of the full pins. The half pins should be almost as deep as the full pins. An interesting effect can be achieved by making dovetail finger joints on angled or compound-angled drawer or box sides.

Variations of decorative finger joints and dovetails are virtually unlimited. Some examples are presented at right and on the facing page from Hugo Kükelhaus's book, *Werde Tischler* ("To Be a Cabinetmaker"; 1953).

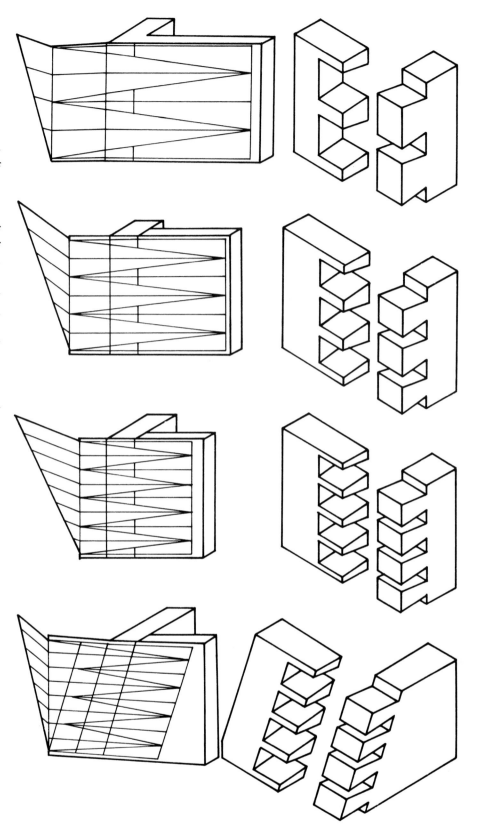

Decorative dovetail designs (from Hugo Kükelhaus's book, Werde Tischler, *1953)*

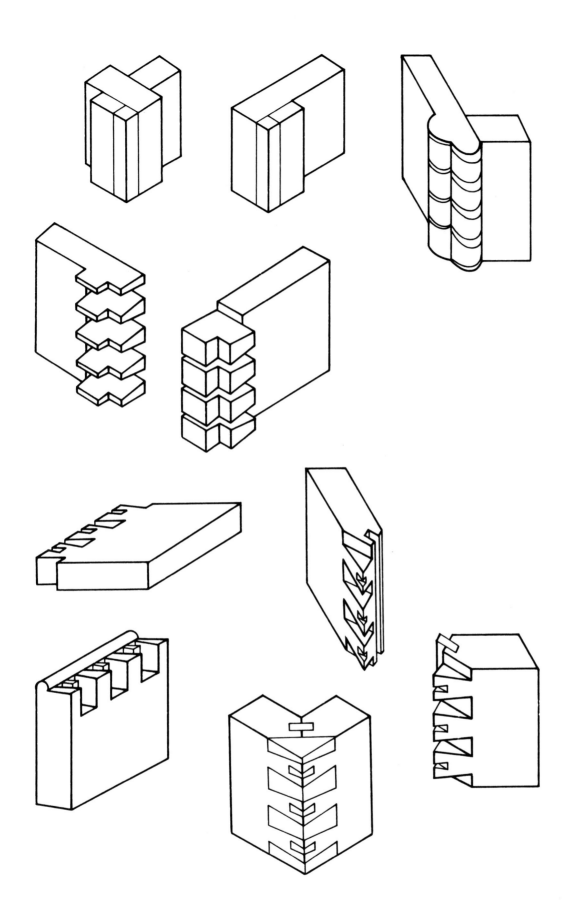

Treenails and Dowels

Treenails have been used in cabinet-making and carpentry for hundreds of years, and they still play an important role today. They serve well as fasteners on frame furniture, board furniture and solid chairs, and also as reinforcement for glued slip joints. On unglued slip joints for outdoor furniture, treenails are indispensable. They withstand moisture and acidity much better than metal fasteners.

In timber-frame construction, tenoned ties and braces require treenails to provide the necessary resistance to tension. These frame-stiffening elements lose their effectiveness if not pinned. Lap joints must also be fastened with treenails.

Treenails are square-cut from dry willow, birch or basswood (timber framers prefer oak or ash). They should be slightly larger in diameter than the hole, with two opposite corners stop-chamfered (as shown in the top drawing at right), so that their edges cut into the sides of the hole and remain in place through friction. The treenail's thickest section should be driven parallel to the grain, to avoid splitting the wood. In cabinetmaking applications, the end of the treenail should be beveled, especially if is to be glued.

When used to pin lap joints, treenails should be made with parallel sides and the holes should be angled, not perpendicular.

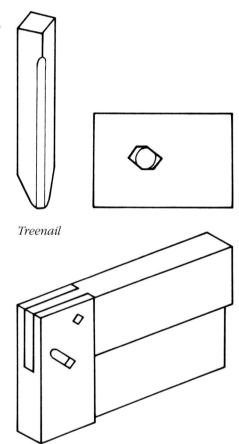

Treenail

Slip joint pinned with treenails

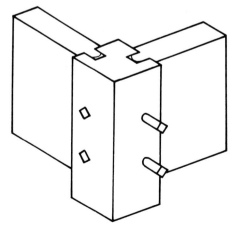

Tongue-and-groove corner joint pinned with treenails

When used to pin slip joints, treenails should be tapered toward the end. In this application, the holes through the mortise cheeks are drilled first, then the tenon is fitted. With the tenon in place, the tenon cheek is marked with an awl through the holes in the mortise side. With the tenon removed, the marks are offset slightly toward the shoulder, and the holes are drilled. When the tapered treenails are driven home in the reassembled joint, the offset holes will seat the tenon firmly in the mortise.

The holes should be as close to the shoulder as possible, so that the tenon does not split.

Dowels are similar to treenails, except that they are always round, usually have chamfered ends and are often grooved to ensure better glue adhesion.

Wooden dowels have been important joint fasteners since time immemorial, especially for tables, chairs and beds. The use of modern doweling machines has extended their field of application. For example, they are used on light frames that are too narrow to be tenoned. If dowels are used on mitered frames, they should be located close to the inner corner to reduce the risk of split-out.

The dowel, which is essentially an easy-to-use loose tenon, is particularly well suited for the manufacture of mass-produced furniture, because it greatly reinforces the simple glued butt joint. If dowels are used to splice boards along their length, the mating surfaces of the butt joint should be angled to ensure a stronger glue joint. However, doweled splicing joints, though cheap and easy to make, are the weakest kind of splice.

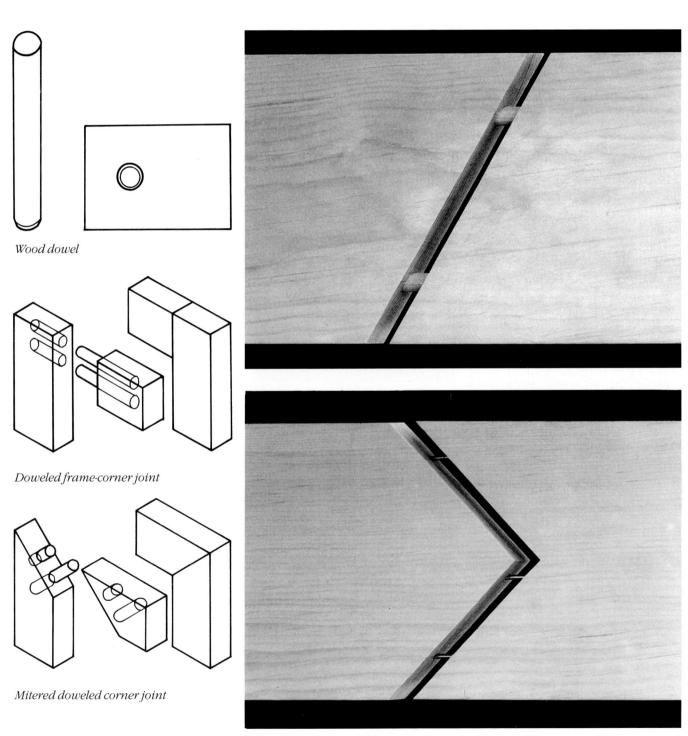

Wood dowel

Doweled frame-corner joint

Mitered doweled corner joint

Splicing joints pinned with wood dowels and metal rods
(Kakushi-da-bo-saba-tsugi/Kakushi-da-bo-ko-sa-tsuki-awase-tsugi)

Butterfly Keys

Butterfly keys (also known as **dovetail keys)** are excellent fasteners for joints that must later be disassembled. They hold joint surfaces together effectively, but they cannot withstand bending or twisting. In recent times, butterfly keys have been largely superseded by metal fasteners.

Butterfly keys are still used fairly extensively in Japan to lock mitered frames and edge-join boards.

The keys can be glued when used in interior applications. The round-headed key is a popular variation, because the hollows can be bored easily with a knot-plugging machine or a Forstner-type drill bit.

Butterfly key (Chi-giri-iri-o-dome-tsugi)

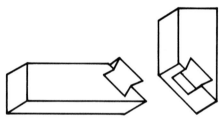

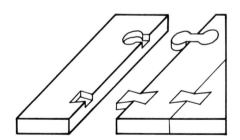

Perpendicular butterfly key

Spline Inserts

Splines of plywood, fiberboard or even cross-grain wood (preferably maple) are used primarily to reinforce corner joints on frames. These joints are similar to the spline-and-groove joints discussed on p. 125. On mitered corner joints, the grooves for the spline must be cut close to the inside corner so that they don't weaken the joint.

A variation on the simple spline insert is the elliptical Lamello biscuit, or joining plate. The biscuits are easily and quickly installed in slots cut with a special plate joiner.

Long-grain splines and **cross-grain splines** reinforce longer edges. Splines with longitudinal grain should be made from wood with spiral grain so that they will be less likely to split out or shear.

Spline miters, which are similar to the Japanese *Shachi-sen* keys (see p. 144), are inserted diagonally across the grain. When glued, they provide a surprisingly strong joint. They can be installed in either diagonal direction, depending on whether the inside or the outside of the joint is to be visible (see the top left photos on p. 144). Splines can also be used unglued to prevent flush, parallel boards from moving out of alignment as a result of warpage, for example between soffit boards.

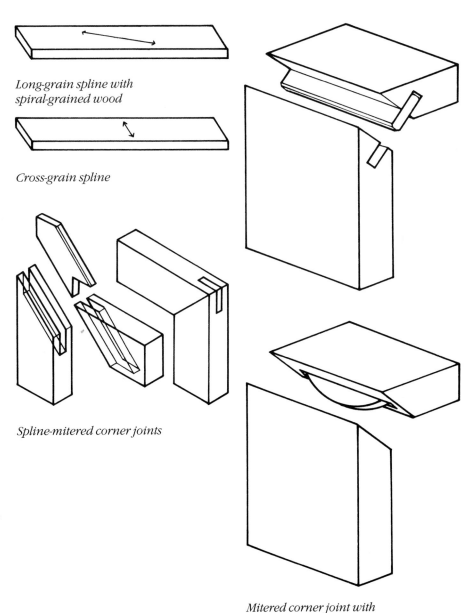

Long-grain spline with spiral-grained wood

Cross-grain spline

Spline-mitered corner joints

Mitered corner joint with Lamello biscuit

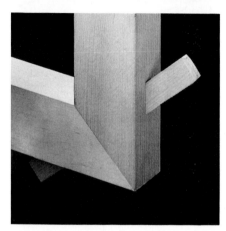

Mitered joints with splines (Shachi-sen)

(Hako-dome-sen-tsugi)

Japanese Treenails, Keys and Wedges

In Japan, treenails, keys and wedges play an important role in preventing joints from slipping and in increasing tension resistance. Various applications of these fastening devices have been illustrated throughout this book. The Japanese classify them as follows:

Dabo, a simple square peg, or treenail, which is used as a blind connection between timbers placed on top of each other, such as between sills and floor beams, or between the mating members of a tabled scarf joint.

Shachi-sen is a rectangular key used to lock spliced timbers, similar to the one used in the West to form splined beams. In Japan, it is used primarily in rod mortise-and-tenon joints, where it is inserted diagonal to grain direction, and as a spline or feather across mitered joints (see the photos at top left).

Komi-sen, or ***Dai-sen,*** are square, tapered treenails used to peg tabled scarf joints.

Kogai-sen is a strong, square key used, for example, to prevent paneling boards from slipping sideways on their dovetail backing boards as a result of wood shrinkage.

Hana-sen is a wedge-shaped key used to secure projecting through tenons.

Wariku-sabi are wedges driven into the end grain of through tenons, forcing the tenons to spread into a dovetail shape.

Yoko-sen is a spline used to secure butt-jointed timbers that carry little load, especially if the timbers will subsequently be enclosed.

Kusabi are wedges used in timber framing to secure tenons in their mortises.

Tenon splines

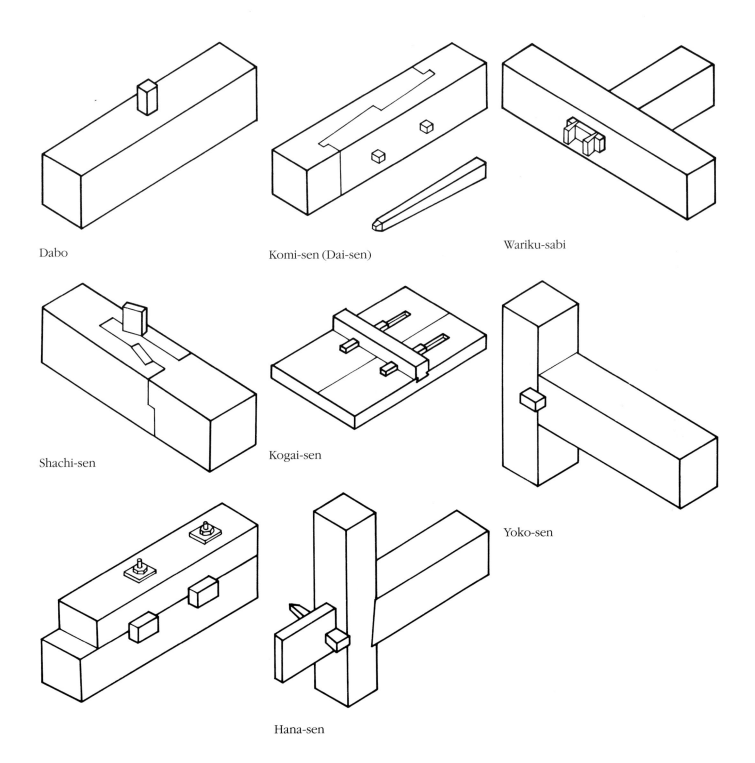

Dabo

Komi-sen (Dai-sen)

Wariku-sabi

Shachi-sen

Kogai-sen

Yoko-sen

Hana-sen

Appendix

Classification of European Wood Joints

In Europe, joints are usually classified according to the position of the mating members:

    1. Splicing joints

    2. Corner joints between timbers of equal width

    3. Lap joints in which the top surfaces of the crossed members are flush

    4. Cogged joints, assembled on corners or as a cross, in which the top surfaces of the mating members are not flush

    5. Oblique joints

    6. Edge joints between boards or timbers

Classification of Japanese Wood Joints

The Japanese classify wood joints into two main categories:

    1. Edge joints between flat boards (types A to D)

    2. Joints between timbers that are square or approximately square in section (types E to H)

Type A
Hagia-wase 矧合
Parallel or corner joints for increasing the width of boards in the same plane; often glued

Type B
Hirauchi-tsugi 平打接
Right-angled carcase joints for furniture, often in the form of mortise-and-tenon joints

Type C
Hashi-bame-tsugi 端嵌接
End-grain edging to prevent warpage

Type D
Kumite-tsugi 組手接
Finger joints, corresponding to Western dovetail joints, for joining boards at any angle

Type E
Tome-tsugi 留接
Corner joints between square timbers that are mitered to hide the end grain

Type F
Ai-gaki-tsugi 相欠接
Right-angled half-lap joints

Type G
Hozo-tsugi 枘接
Right-angled mortise (*hozoana*) and tenon (*hozo*) joints

Type H
Tsugite 継手
Splicing joints for lengthening timbers

The table at right (which is continued on pp. 148-149) shows how this system of classification corresponds to the Japanese joints depicted in this book.

Page			Type
31	錆交叉接	Saba-ko-sa-tsugi	H
36	四方鯱組手	Shi-ho-shachi-kumi-te	H
38	鯱継	Shachi-tsugi	H
41	十文字継手	Jyu-mon-ji-tsugi-te	H
42	蟻継手	Ari-tsugi-te	H
43	二枚蟻接	Ni-mai-ari-tsugi	A
43	両面蟻継	Ryo-men-ari-tsugi	H
44	鎌継	Kama-tsugi	H
45	芒継	Noge-tsugi	H
46	両杵型継	Ryo-kine-gata-tsugi	H
47	四方鎌継	Shi-ho-kama-tsugi	H
50	台接継手	Daimochi-tsugi-te	H
51	追掛大栓継	Okkake-dai-sen-tsugi	H
56	貫四方差し	Nuki-shiho-zashi	H
57	矩形相欠接	Kane-gata-ai-gaki-tsugi	F
58	金輪継	Kana-wa-tsugi	H
59	二面金輪大栓継	Ni-men-kana-wa-dai-sen-tsugi-te	H
59	二面金輪鯱栓継	Ni-men-kana-wa-shachi-sen-tsugi-te	H
60	二方鯱栓	Ni-ho-shachi-sen	H
61	二方大栓継手	Ni-ho-dai-sen-tsugi-te	H
61	箱継鯱栓	Hako-tsugite-shachi-sen	H
79	燧蟻落とし	Hiuchi-ari-otoshi	H

Index

Publisher: John Kelsey
Translator: James Rudstrom
Editor: Peter Chapman
Layout artist: Jodie Delohery
Illustrator: Louise Oldenbourg (except where noted)
Photographer: Walter Grunder (except where noted)

Typeface: Garamond
Paper: Warren Patina Matte, 70 lb., neutral pH
Printer and binder: Arcata Graphics, Kingsport, Tennessee